Hercules' Labours

Cover photograph by kind permission of the
Museum of Fine Arts, Boston

The Andokides Painter
The Lysippides Painter
Two-handled jar (amphora) with Herakles driving a bull to
sacrifice (detail)
Greek, Archaic Period, about 525-520 B.C.
Place of Manufacture: Greece, Attica, Athens
Ceramic, Black Figure and Red Figure (Bilingual)
Height: 53.2 cm (20 15/16 in.)
Museum of Fine Arts, Boston
Henry Lillie Pierce Fund, 99.538
Photograph © 2007 Museum of Fine Arts, Boston

This book and others available at
www.treetongue.co.uk

Hercules' Labours

The Evolutionary Path round the Horoscope

Phoebe Wyss

Tree Tongue Publishing
www.treetongue.co.uk

Published by Tree Tongue
2 Chapel Downs Cottages
Threshers
Crediton
Devon
EX 17 3PB

ISBN 0-954-6099-6-4

About the Author

Phoebe left an academic career to become an astrologer. After university, with an MA in English (University of Reading) she went to Germany where she held a post as Lektorin at Hanover University for twenty years. Astrology, however, had always been her passion, and in 1985 she gave up teaching English to become a full-time astrologer. From 1985-96 she worked in Germany counselling, teaching astrology classes, holding workshops, and giving public talks. Her astrological board game *'Lebensrad'* was published there in 1986. 1993 saw the publication of a second board game *'Die Wendeltreppe'* and *'Das Orakelbuch'* (Burk Verlag). In 1997 she returned to England, and since then has been working as an astrologer in Hove. She founded the Brighton and Hove Astrology Circle in 2005, which runs a programme of weekly meetings. Phoebe is also a meditator on the Osho path, and feels that her 30-year practical experience of personal and spiritual development has enriched her astrology.

See www.astrophoebe.com

Contents

Preface to the Reader Unversed in Astrology

Although this looks like an astrology book, it is also for readers without a knowledge of astrology who are on a spiritual path, as its subject is the growth of consciousness. Astrology is used here as a tool to increase awareness. It is the best thing around for making us conscious of our patterns that manifest in what we do, say, feel and think. It also helps us understand the significance of our life experience by putting it in wider contexts of meaning.

So in this book astrology provides a map for determining where you are, where you have come from and where you are going. It is used to reveal your spiritual itinerary - the specific challenges on your personal life agenda, and the order in which you will meet them.

You need to know three facts only from your birth chart in order to apply the interpretations in the different chapters to your own life and then you're ready to go. They are:

1 the house of the sun in your chart
2 the house of Saturn in your chart
3 the house in your chart that Saturn is transiting at present

If you have not got a personal birth chart, you can obtain one free online at www.astro.com. Request your chart to be drawn using the equal house system. Then, knowing these three facts, you can turn to the chapters that have relevance for you personally.

The chapter on the house of your sun will describe the personality qualities that can help or hinder you in performing your labours. The chapter on the house of your natal Saturn, meaning Saturn in your birth chart, will describe your life-long karmic labour. The house of transiting Saturn, meaning where Saturn is at present in your chart, will describe your current area of challenge.

And, when you know that Saturn takes about two and a half years to move through each house, you will be able to look into the future to see where he is heading, and read the corresponding chapter in advance to get some tips. Or you can revisit your past by looking retrospectively at the chapters on the challenges you have already faced, which will help you integrate your experience.

Unless otherwise indicated, the statements about Saturn in a specific house apply both when your natal Saturn is there, and when Saturn is there in transit. Natal Saturn and transiting Saturn stand for the same archetype so, when they are in the same energy field, the time factor is the only difference. Saturn in transit represents a transient state that passes after a couple of years, but Saturn's house position in your birth chart is relevant for your whole life.

Also, when expressions such as 'a first-house person' or 'a second-house person' are used, those with a first or second-house sun are referred to in the first instance. But also included are those readers who have these houses emphasised through the placement of a number of other planets there.

When expressions such as 'in the first house' or 'in the second house' are used, what is being described is especially relevant to those who have reached these respective houses on their journey round the wheel - either natally or due to their current Saturn transit.

Although this book lends itself to 'pick and mix' reading, the chapters should also be read in their sequence for the reader to experience the twelve-staged development of spiritual understanding that the houses present. Meaning in the wheel is cumulative, and thus the themes of the earlier chapters are simple compared to those of the later ones. We find that, as we progress round the wheel, the subject matter becomes deeper, and psychologically and spiritually more complex.

Preface to the Reader
Versed in Astrology

The approach to the astrological houses used in this book is archetypal in that the houses are seen as expressions of the same twelve archetypes as lie behind the signification of the signs. This implies close correspondences between the two wheels of the horoscope. In fact, houses are described here as if they were signs, making this a 'sun-house' rather than a 'sun-sign' book. Seeing the houses as having their roots in the twelve zodiacal archetypes, does not contradict classical house signification, but deepens and enriches it.

In experimenting with this approach, I aim to expand our understanding experientially of what the houses stand for, and invite readers to test whether the issues presented here, when applied to their personal charts, can be related to their personality and life.

The astrological houses have been an area of contention for the last two thousand years - in fact ever since being separated from the signs in western astrology and presented as something different. Not only have more than a hundred different methods of house division been invented as a consequence, but there is disagreement among astrologers about what the houses stand for in real terms.

For example, astrologers who practice traditional astrology (the astrology inherited from ancient Greece via the Arabs and William Lilly) interpret the houses as distinct from the signs, as they believe their signification developed independently.[1] However, in twentieth century psychological astrology the similarities between signs and houses have been recognised.[2] Although I prefer to call the kind of astrology I practice transpersonal rather than psychological, I agree with the latter view. In my experience using a close correspondence between signs and houses works.

Instead of arguing about which approach is right, I suggest we see traditional and psychological astrology as two separate disciplines that come from different traditions, each with its own approach and techniques. The origin of traditional astrology lies in ancient divination practices, used for political purposes or for private fortune-telling,[3] whereas psychological and transpersonal astrology are rooted in the spiritual practices of the ancient mystery schools. Their focus is on self-discovery and self-knowledge for personal development and spiritual growth.

I see my approach as transpersonal, believing as I do that the patterns of meaning that form astrology's subject matter derive from a higher source than the human mind. This view is supported by Richard Tarnas in his recently published book *Cosmos and Psyche* that expands our

1 Deborah Houlding *The Houses Temples of the Sky* (The Wessex Astrologer, Bournemouth 2006)

2 Howard Sasportas *The Twelve Houses* (The Aquarian Press, Wellingborough 1985)

3 Geoffrey Cornelius *The Moment of Astrology* (The Wessex Astrologer, Bournemouth 2003)

understanding of the archetypes by describing the way they manifest throughout history.[4] He proves convincingly that, rather than being projections of the human mind, they are embedded in the ground of the vast cosmic processes that govern not only human life but also pattern evolution in a universal sense.

In fact the archetypes can be seen as the basic structural ideas in the anima mundi, or mind of God. Seen from the perspective of the new physics, this universal mind is similar to, or identical with, the quantum flow that forms the ground of both matter and mind and contains the matrix of creation.

I imagine an archetype as being the 'magnetic' centre of a field or cluster of related ideas and potential meaning. These can become manifest and take form as phenomena, for example when they are activated at a certain stage in a time cycle, or else remain latent. This is not a mechanical process, however, governed by the law of cause and effect. The universal mind is alive, conscious and in continual flux, and as the universe is in a process the future remains open.

This means that only tendencies or likelihoods, depending on which archetype is being activated, can be foreseen. The exact prediction of events is not possible because, although it follows consistent patterns of the highest coherence and order, the universal mind is free to be spontaneously creative.

---

4 Richard Tarnas *Cosmos and Psyche* (Viking, New York, 2006)

Following Saturn's cycle to the ascendant, this book will take you on a journey through the twelve zodiacal archetypes as symbolised by the houses in the birth chart. Each house is like a field of potentiality out of which issues from a specific range of subject matter can manifest. It is structured round one of mythology's most famous accounts of the archetypal journey of a hero, and is also the story of our lives.

Although they lend themselves to 'pick and mix' reading, the chapters in this book should also be read in their sequence for the reader to experience the twelve-staged development of spiritual understanding that the houses present. Meaning in the wheel is cumulative, and thus the themes of the earlier chapters are simple compared to those of the later ones. So we find that, as we progress round the wheel, the subject matter becomes deeper, and psychologically and spiritually more complex.

Introduction

The Soul of the Universe speaks through Myth

Following in the footsteps of Alice Bailey,[1] I take up the myth of Hercules again to use the story of his twelve labours as an allegory for the evolutionary path of spiritual development. The new paradigm of reality now emerging is similar to that of the ancients in that it reveals an ensouled universe. The gods are back again and are now called archetypes. Jung, who developed our modern understanding of archetypes, saw them as structural ideas within the ground of the collective unconscious. In the context of the new physics, we can understand this ground as the quantum flow that underlies both matter and mind.

We also know from modern science that there is fractal mirroring on every scale of size in the universe. This allows us to embrace once more the ancient axiom of 'as above so below', and see ourselves as a microcosm of the macrocosm. Like us, the whole then has both an outer material sheath and an inner life. It appears conscious, with a mind and a creative imagination expressing meaning and moral purpose.

The quantum flow investigated by today's physicists is very like the stream of consciousness of a universal mind. Within it lie formative ideas that give structure, and out of it new ideas are born continuously. Some of these remain on the level of mind, while others manifest in material reality.

---

1 Alice Bailey was the first to allot each labour to a sign of the zodiac in *The Labours of Hercules: An Astrological Interpretation* (Lucis Publishing Company).

As the universe is one interconnected whole on all levels, we can envisage our individual minds as participating in the universal mind. Then, because our consciousness is its consciousness, and our will contributes to the will of the whole, we must see ourselves as co-creators with a power to determine what comes to pass. There is also communication between the whole and the part, and the great universal myths and symbols can be seen as vehicles through which the whole speaks to us. The universal mind reveals its moral purpose through them, and through them demonstrates the patterns of meaning in our human experience. Astrology is the best tool we have for discerning these patterns, as it reveals how they manifest in history and in our individual lives.

So, in the context of this thinking, which is still new and not yet accepted by the mainstream, I have taken the myths of Hercules labours and interpreted them astrologically. In doing so, I have followed Alice Bailey's allocation of each myth to a specific astrological principle. Through referring to their birth charts, readers will hear the archetypes speaking to them personally. And the times when their relevance is likely to emerge in their individual lives is indicated through using the Saturn cycle as a measure.

The Prototype Hero

Hercules, prototype of the mythological hero, was an illegitimate son of Zeus, who kept mixing his genes with humankind by seducing mortal women. Half son of god but also son of man, Hercules inherits human blindness, and makes mistakes for which he then must pay.

His biggest mistake comes at the beginning of the story when, either drunk or in a rage and therefore not in his right mind, he slays his wife and children. Hercules, like us, goes astray when he is unconscious and knows not what he is doing. After he comes to his senses, he is wracked with remorse and seeks an audience with his father. Zeus comes up with a plan of how he can absolve his karma. He must be bound in service to King Eurystheus of Mycenae, and serve him obediently until the debt has been paid.

This king then uses his chance of having the greatest strongman of antiquity at his command, and sends Hercules off to perform a series of mind-boggling tasks. Thus Hercules must face the twelve challenges that will be the making of him. At the beginning of the story he is little more than a foolhardy, uncouth lout, but as he progresses he learns and grows, showing great strengths of character - undaunted courage, the readiness to take risks and a willingness to serve. On returning triumphant, he is celebrated by the people as their hero, having risked his life again and again for the common good.

So, if you are looking for a role model, why not take Hercules? He always remains positive, even when faced with seemingly impossible tasks, and he has sticking power. He stays on track till each labour is completed, and he is open to new, creative solutions as shown by his sudden brainwaves. Finally, in his unquenchable thirst for adventure, he is a shining example to us all of how to live life to the fullest.

The Wheel of Life

The story of Hercules' labours is presented here as a journey round the wheel of life. From the earliest cultures known to us change was observed to move in cycles, and time has been depicted as a wheel with four, eight or twelve spokes. The wheel of the solar year with its four seasons has four spokes marking the equinoxes and solstices (Fig. 1). The ancient image of the eight-spoked wheel of Vishnu's chariot (Fig. 2, overleaf) includes the addition of the mid-season peaks, creating a total of eight high points in the year. These were celebrated as religious festivals.[2] Timing them correctly was the work of the astronomer-astrologers, who would record the eight relevant positions of the rising sun around the horizon using natural landscape features, or by erecting standing stones.

A human life can be seen as one round of the wheel. In Fig. 3 the four ages of man are drawn progressing anticlockwise in line with the sequence of the houses in a horoscope. Our lives are governed by the vast pattern of interlocking cycles created by the planets that continuously encircle us. And just as the eight sunrise positions accrued different meanings in ancient cultures, so the different stages of the cycles of the planets have each their own significance.

2 See Peter Dawkins' interpretation of the wheel of life in *Zoence: the Science of Life* (Samuel Weiser, Inc York Beach, Maine 1998)

Fig. 1   The Wheel of the Solar Year

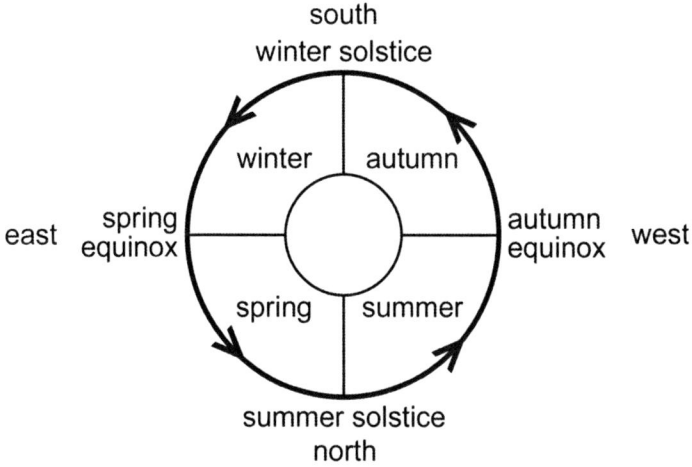

Fig. 3   The Wheel of Life

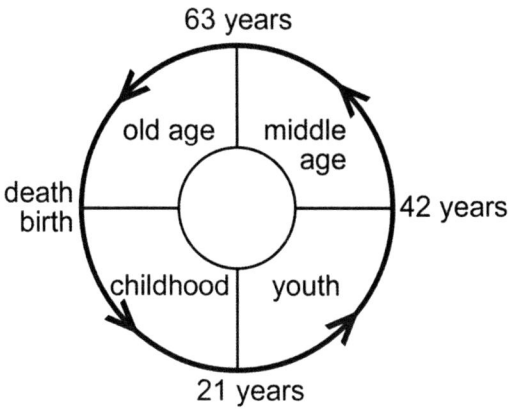

Introduction

The daily path of the sun has always been used to measure time. In early cultures sticks were erected to cast moving shadows and create sundials. The sun appears to move because, due to the earth turning on its axis, the whole wheel of the sky is seen revolving once around us in twenty-four hours, causing the rising, culminating and setting of the sun, moon and stars over our local horizon. The different stages of the sun's diurnal cycle are represented in a horoscope by the houses, each having a traditional meaning.

Fig. 2   The wheel of Vishnu's chariot

In modern western horoscopy, earth and sky are drawn as two wheels with twelve spokes each. In Fig. 4 they are combined so that Aries, the first sign, falls on the first house, but the wheels can align with each other in any other way, depending on the time of day for which the horoscope is being drawn.

Fig. 4   A Two-wheeled Horoscope Diagram with corresponding Signs and Houses

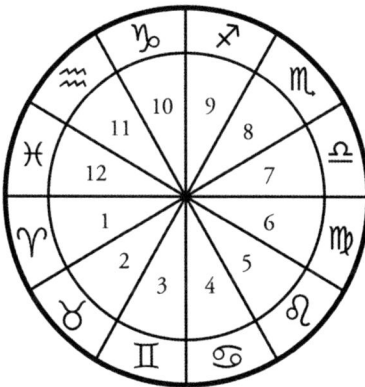

Of all the planetary cycles the twenty-nine-year cycle of Saturn to the birth chart ascendant[3] is the most relevant to the myth of Hercules' labours, so this is the cycle we will be focusing on (Fig. 5, overleaf).

---

3 The Ascendant in a birth chart is the degree of the sign on the Eastern horizon at the time of birth.

Fig. 5 The Saturn Cycle

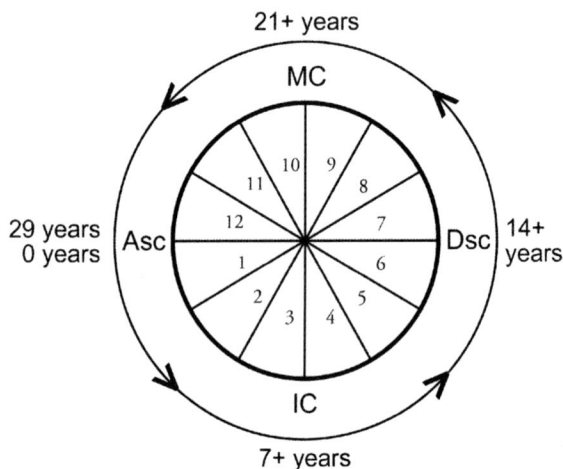

21+ years

MC

29 years
0 years | Asc

Dsc | 14+
years

IC

7+ years

What are the Houses Exactly?

The signs of the zodiac stand for the twelve basic archetypal principles that have their source in the universal mind, or the mind of God. Ancient esoteric teaching speaks of twelve cosmic energies or rays that manifest on all levels of creation, and can be compared to twelve different colours, each resonating at its own frequency. These frequencies can be distinguished by heightened human senses and experienced, for example, as different energies within a personality - which is why sensitive amateurs are often good at guessing people's sun signs.

In a horoscope diagram the twelve archetypal principles are represented in both the wheel of the signs and in the wheel of the houses. In each wheel they appear in the same sequence and with the same internal geometric patterning, reflecting the mathematics intrinsic to what is called 'sacred geometry'. Thus, as the two wheels mirror each other in the sequence and inter-relationships of the archetypes, the houses should be approached in the same way as the signs. We gain insight into the nature of the archetype behind a house by knowing the characteristics of its corresponding sign - its element, its triplicity and its ruling planet - all of which add dimension to our understanding of a house's meaning.[4]

The sign corresponding to the house of our sun will contribute its colour to our personality and its issues to our life themes. Sometimes its archetype will be clearly manifested in our physical appearance. The house of our moon, and the houses of other personal planets are also relevant, but these can be put aside for the moment as secondary factors.

Therefore on an energy level there is no difference between the two wheels, although in other respects they vary. For example, the houses of the inner wheel are drawn in the same position in every chart, aligning with the horizon and the compass directions, and with the first house in the east (Fig. 4). The signs on the outer wheel, however, are divisions of the wheel of the sky that revolves around us, and therefore change their positions from minute to minute in relation to the horizon. Thus it is important, when we draw a birth chart, to know the time

---

4 See table in Appendix II.

of birth as accurately as possible in order to align the two wheels correctly.[5]

So what are the houses exactly? In the first instance they represent local space. They are a division of the circle of the earth and sky surrounding us into twelve sections. We could imagine twelve standing stones erected round the horizon marking twelve compass directions, and these would then correspond to our house cusps (the dividing lines between the houses in a chart). Perhaps it is because the houses represent the earth in the first instance that, in contrast to the signs, their themes have traditionally more to do with areas of earthly life.

In ancient cultures each compass direction was believed to be ruled by a specific god. For example, in India there were eight guardians of space including Indra who ruled the east, Varuna who ruled the west, and Kubera and Yama who ruled the north and south respectively. The personalities of these gods influenced the energy of the directions, affecting the sun, moon and planets as they passed through.

I believe that the mythology of the directions flowed into the signification of the astrological houses as passed down to us from antiquity. For example, in the Vedic culture Saturn was the ruler of the west, which may explain the dark themes attributed to the eighth house,

---

5 A good book for learning natal charting is John Filby's *Natal Charting* (The Aquarian Press, Wellingborough 1981).

also why the seventh house is the house of open enemies and why Saturn is exalted in Libra.[6]

Time and Planetary Cycles

The astrologer plots the courses of the planets as they weave their cycles in time and studies the unfolding of their respective archetypes. Within the range of meaning of each archetype lies the key to the significance of what is happening and may happen in our lives. What manifests, however, depends in the first instance on the phase we are in of the respective cycle.

All cosmic processes show alternating phases of expansion and contraction, which can be compared to breathing in and breathing out. In her expansion phase between the winter and summer solstices, nature breathes in, and then breathes out again as the light wanes from summer peak to winter nadir. Or, during the monthly lunar cycle, the energy on our planet expands when the moon is waxing and we gain ground in our projects. But, after the waxing phase has peaked at full moon, contraction starts and we lose ground while the moon is waning.

The cycle of Saturn to the ascendant, divided into twelve stages by the houses, also falls into two parts. The lower hemisphere in a chart, the haunt of the sun at night corresponding to the underworld, is where we breathe in,

---

6 See Phoebe Wyss *The Spin of the Wheel* (The Astrological Journal Vol. 49, Number 1). Also on www.astrophoebe.com.

whereas we breathe out in the daytime half of the wheel. So our labours in the houses below the horizon will have a different focus to our labours in the houses above it.

The fourteen-and-a-half-year period of Saturn's passage through the first six houses on the wheel is a time of incubation in our lives during which we grow internally. We develop our strengths, accumulate power and create our necessary security structures. Then, when Saturn crosses the descendant and enters the upper hemisphere, it is time to flower. Before us lies our out-breath period. We have fourteen and a half years to give out what we have taken in, to share our talents and use the strengths we have developed to make our contribution (Fig. 5).

Fig. 6   The Four Quadrants

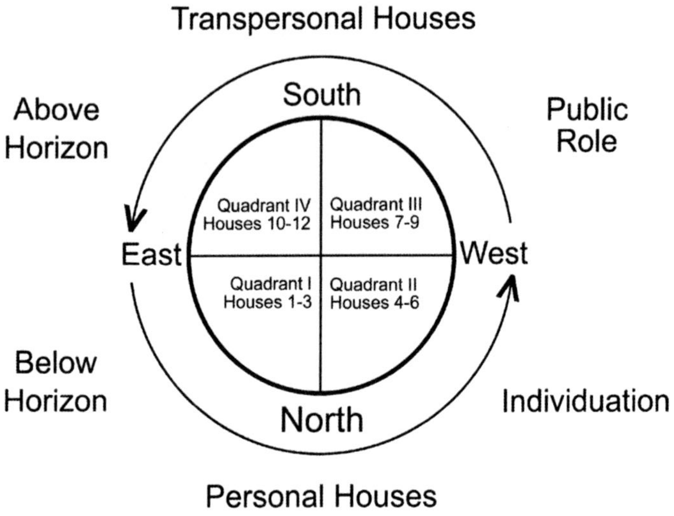

The lines of the horizon and meridian form a cross that further divides the inner wheel into four groups of three houses called quadrants (Fig. 6). The quadrants reflect the quadruplicities (the four elements). We can also divide the wheel into what I call 'trigants', which are based on the triplicities - three groups of four houses (Fig. 7). These areas, created by the energetic patterning within the wheel, have different ranges of significance.[7] So the focus of our labours changes as we pass from one group of houses into the next.

Fig. 7   The Three Trigants

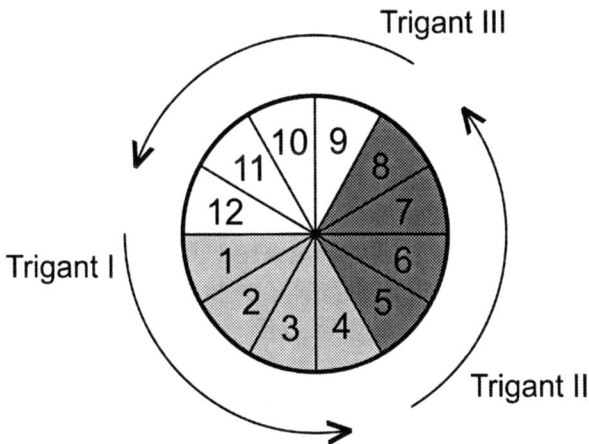

7 The meaning of these groupings is well described by Howard Sasportas in *The Twelve Houses* (The Aquarian Press 1985)

Saturn in the Role of King Eurystheus

Since psychological astrology remodelled Saturn from medieval malefic into our wisest teacher,[8] we have been able to see the hardships he brings in a positive light as learning situations. If we are playing Hercules, Saturn has been cast in the role of King Eurystheus. He will put us in difficult situations that stretch us to our limits, or imprison us in constricting circumstances, giving us the choice to either grow inwardly or to curl up and die.

Thank God we have astrology to explain what is going on! Astrology's explanatory power helps us determine which lessons we are currently supposed to be learning, allowing us to take a peep at our syllabus. We can use it to follow Saturn's transit path round our chart, and identify where the pressure will next be brought to bear. Once we have identified the archetypes that are about to be activated, we will know the sort of thing to expect.

As he progresses round the wheel, Saturn brings our problems to a head in the areas of our life represented by the houses. In each in turn the heat is turned up, and, try though we may, we cannot escape because Saturn has nailed us down. Then the status quo we have been putting up with starts to feel so suffocating that we become desperate to change it.

After some failed attempts, we may finally understand what really needs to be changed - and that is our consciousness. It is not the situation itself but the way we look

---

8 Liz Greene *Saturn: a new Look at an old Devil* (Samuel Weiser New York 1976)

at it that makes it unbearable. And if we change our viewpoint we will find everything has changed. So it seems that Saturn has honourable intentions - that he leads us into pain and difficulty in order to shake us awake. His transits then turn out to be opportunities to notch our consciousness up one peg higher. We are too uncomfortable to remain drowsy and on automatic pilot, so we have to wake up - either briefly or for ever.

This book presents Hercules' labours as a spiritual path, whereby spirituality is understood in a modern post-secular way. The challenges Hercules faces are metaphors for the challenges confronting us on our journey through life. The monsters he wrestles with dwell in our minds. They are projections of our fears, our negativity and our destructiveness. In fact they are what has been preventing us from taking our seat on Mount Olympus, and realising our true nature as a god among gods.

So, dear reader, you are now invited to embark on a journey round the wheel of life in Hercules' footsteps and with Saturn as your guide, whereby your itinerary decrees that you visit each house in turn, starting with the first, and that you continue undeterred until you have completed all of your twelve labours.

The First House

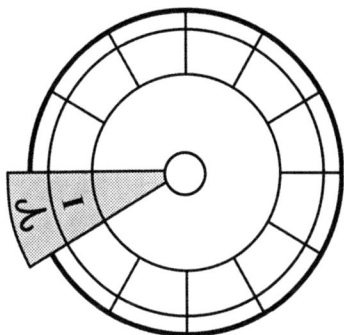

Taming the Wild Mares of Diomedes

Hercules must serve King Eurystheus for twelve years to atone for killing his wife and children. His first labour is to capture the man-eating mares of Diomedes, the leader of a warlike tribe. When he arrives in their territory, Hercules overpowers the men who guard the horses and begins driving them away. But he is pursued by Diomedes in his chariot together with a band of warriors. To be free to fight them, Hercules entrusts the mares to a youth named Abderos. But the mares get the better of Abderos and kill him. Meanwhile Hercules has slain Diomedes, and put his army to flight. Then, harnessing a team of mares to the chariot, he rides home in it, driving the rest of the horses before him. His great feat is celebrated, but Abderos lies dead.

The Lonely Hero

Our journey round the wheel of the houses begins at the ascendant on the eastern horizon - the point symbolising birth that is touched each year at the spring equinox by the rising sun. Here the source of our cosmic power supply is found. As long as we are plugged in, energy flows from this place into our system, charging our batteries and filling us with vitality.

Let us get our bearings. We are at the first corner of the fire trine (Fig. 8), which is also the first point of the cardinal cross (Fig. 9). Thus the energy form of the first house is cardinal fire - the most dynamic type of cosmic energy. The cardinal cross is formed in the wheel of the houses by the four angular houses standing for four primary areas of life. The first house equates with self and

Fig. 8   The Fire Trine

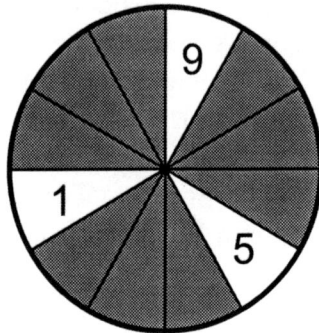

identity, the fourth with home and family, the seventh with marriage and partnerships and the tenth with career and public standing. The fire trine links the first, the fifth and the ninth house to create a great triangle spanning the wheel.

If you have a first-house sun, whatever sign it is in, you will have a side that is like an Aries. That means, unless there are contra indications such as the presence in the first house of counter-weights like Neptune, or aspects from the sun to him, you will be able to assert yourself strongly. You will always know what you want, and go for it no holds barred. Spontaneous, fearless and quick off the mark, you are the prototype of a self-motivated self-starter.

Fig. 9   The Cardinal Cross

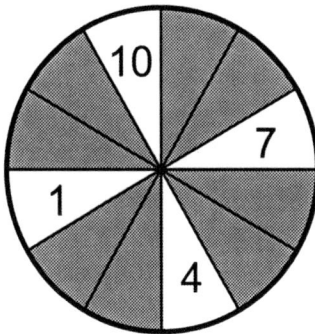

Although others may find you overbearing and too pushy, they will appreciate your authenticity - at least they know where they are with you. And you have an innocent, childlike charm that wins hearts. However, although you may make an outward show of power and confidence, inside you could still feel weak and insecure.

Things work out fine as long as you go it alone and do things your way, but when you have to co-operate with others there is trouble. You are too uncompromising and too confrontational. You get impatient when you are held up, and lose your temper when things go wrong. No wonder people take offence when you tread on their toes and then blame them for being in the way - and you never apologise.

So partnerships are not your thing. Hercules' co-operation with Abderis did not work out either. He overestimated the youth's strength and this led to Abderis' death. Thus Hercules had to learn from the outset that his labours must be performed alone, without assistance from others. A first-house hero is always a lonely hero.

A Fresh Start

If Saturn has recently crossed your ascendant in transit and arrived in your first house, you may be feeling somewhat crumpled, like a chick newly hatched from an egg. Perhaps you have been thrown by a life-change and you are just struggling to your feet. Perhaps you are discovering that you are all alone now, as the people you relied on for support in the past have vanished.

Don't worry! As he moves forward through the personal part of your chart below the horizon, Saturn will be rehabilitating you step by step, putting your security structures back in place. This process begins in the first house, the house of identity, where your task is to forge a new, more up to date persona. If Saturn is in the first house in your birth chart, this will be a life-long task. If he is there in transit, it will be your task for the next few years. In either case take a long and honest look at yourself in the mirror. Do you know the person reflected there? Does the expression on the face looking back at you correspond to how you feel inside?

One thing is clear in the first house, and that is that we want to make a fresh start. Our old ways of dealing with things are no longer appropriate, and the last thing we want is to repeat the past. So we make a resolution to do things differently from now on. And nothing seems to be standing in our way. The future seen from the perspective of the first house appears open - as if we could do anything or be anything we like - but nevertheless something is holding us back. It is Saturn wheel-clamping us.

When Saturn is in the first house it is as if a load of earth has been thrown onto the cardinal fire that burns there. Our spirit of free enterprise and our enthusiasm for adventure is considerably dampened. We must, however, remember that Saturn is not on the outside. He is inside us, and his voice flagging up cautions is the voice of our own self-doubt and repressed fears. They were always there on a deep level, but now they can well up and inhibit our energy.

The Inner Headmaster

We could be reminded of the time when we were small and wanted to run about, and make a noise and generally let off steam, but we were forced to sit still and shut up. We remember authority figures - parents or teachers - towering over us and enforcing discipline. Together they managed to crush our ebullience, and something in us shut down. That was when we lost the power to express ourself spontaneously.

Before conditioning kicks in, all small children live out each emotion as it arises without inhibition, be it joy, rage, grief or fear. Their self-expression is uninhibited. To be totally self-centred is also their rightful survival mechanism, and they never consider others' needs. When they want something they scream for it whether they disturb their mother, who is asleep, or not. But, as they grow up, children lose their naturalness and become more closed and more inhibited.

The first house that follows the ascendant - the point of birth - is known as the house of infancy, and here we can find ourself regressing to the infantile state. People who otherwise never lose their temper have been known to have temper tantrums like two-year olds in the first house.

When Saturn is there natally, we have probably been on the receiving end of a heavy regime of discipline from an early age. We may have internalised the authority figure who chastised us, and be still carrying him around with us today. He is our inner headmaster, the one who makes sure we keep the rules, and we believe he will come down hard on us if we transgress them. Above all, he is concerned that we control ourselves at all times and in all places.

The man-eating mares represent the anti-social urges and desires that we have repressed. We are, however, uncomfortable with the situation as we are in continual fear of them breaking loose. With all that frustration inside them, they would certainly turn destructive. Thus our wild horses are hobbled, and confined to their stable. With time they get so used to this that they lose their capacity to frisk about freely in unconfined spaces.

But, if it is Saturn who bound us, Saturn is also the one who makes us aware that we are bound. Our chance comes when Saturn is in transit in the first house. Then we become aware of our blocks, and how our life force is no longer flowing so freely. We may notice how physically inhibited, sexually uptight and lacking in spontaneity we have become. And, once we have seen this clearly, we are three-quarters of the way towards changing these patterns.

Know Thyself

It is not easy to take decisive action when Saturn is in the first house. Saturn, always concerned with energy efficiency, tries to prevent us from wasting our efforts through leaping without looking thoroughly first. He has a nasty way of stopping us dead in our tracks by triggering our doubts and fears. Thus he forces us to go in before we go out.

It is clear that the time has come to face our self-defeating beliefs. Not that Saturn puts negativity into our minds, because it was there already deep inside us, but he has his ways of making us conscious of it. So we come face to face with a layer of self-doubt hiding beneath our surface bravado. Deep down, it seems, we are pessimistic about our chances of success, and we are also fearful about having to go it alone. We wish we had someone at our side to give us support, but there is nobody around in the first house, so we are forced to stand on our own feet.

Where did these doubts and fears come from? We may trace them back to our childhood or youth - to situations in which we were harshly judged by some formidable authority figure. When he told us were were no good, and we would never make it, we actually believed him. Worse still, we have made his voice our own, and taken on his role. We do it to ourself now - we put ourself down.

We may also see how we learned to protect ourself from such attacks from the outside. What we did was we erected an invisible wall all around us, behind which we sheltered and where we could remain aloof and untouched. Now, however, with Saturn in our first house, this wall begins to feel oppressive and too confining. It is cutting us off from nourishing contacts with others, and we long to break out.

Part of our labour in the first house will be to dismantle it. This we do by becoming conscious of our automatic defence mechanisms, and then changing the ways we normally react. Thus we open up more to others and to our environment. When nothing awful happens, our trust will grow and our energy level will rise, because, without the wall, the life force can flow freely in both directions.

Thus we reclaim the zest and joie de vivre we enjoyed as small children.

In order to forge a new identity for ourself, we need to know the truth of who we are. So self-inquiry is on our agenda when Saturn is in the first house. His work here is to dispel our illusions, and confront us with the reality of ourself. We all endeavour to look good in front of others, and try to convince them that we are the great person we pretend to be. Slowly we come to believe in the image we have created, and will always try to protect it if it is attacked.

A typical situation is when another person says something negative about our character, and we find ourself getting angry and retaliating with a counter-attack. Afterwards we wonder why we reacted so sensitively. It was because our self-image was under threat and with it our personal security, which is bound up with believing in our positive self-image and getting others to believe in it too.

But, until we accept ourself - warts and all - and find the courage to show ourself as we are, we will remain dependent on others and on their good opinion of us. When Saturn transits our first house, however, we could enter an identity crisis in which the persona that has served us well for so long could crumble. If this happens, it is then a sign that a more honest, up-to-date image of ourself now needs to be created.

Life Abundant is Abundant Energy

The first four houses on the wheel correspond to the four primary bodies - our energy, physical, mental and emotional bodies. In the first house we are working on our energy body - the subtle body, visible to clairvoyants as our aura. If you are puzzled why we look to this house of cardinal fire for information about the physical body, it is because the energy body contains the matrix that determines the form, shape and state of well-being of our material self.

If there are no disturbances in the first house of our chart, our life force will flow unimpeded from our energy body, and our physical body will be strong and healthy. But, if there are disturbances, and the energy is incoherent or blocked, our health and vitality will be affected. Saturn in the first signalises a block. For example, our problem could be that we have a habit of sitting on our energy. This can be exhausting! It is very draining to go on holding strong energy down. So, even though we may not feel like it, we need to keep active and move our energy when Saturn is in the first house, as sitting on the fence will only lead to tension and inner restlessness.

Through all those past millenia when our ancestors were hunters and gatherers, living close to nature and sharing their territory with wild animals, the human body was a primary survival tool. Bodies needed to be strong and fit in those days for a physically arduous life. But our modern lifestyle has assigned the body an unnaturally passive role. No wonder by middle age it begins to look so dead!

When Saturn is in the first house, we can become aware of this, and look for ways of improving our energy flow and increasing our vitality. Modern complementary medicine offers many techniques and treatments that claim to do this, and lead to improved health and well-being. And, when Saturn is in the first, we will have the necessary discipline to keep going with a nutritious diet, or with a programme of physical exercise.

To sum up, our first-house challenge is to channel the strong energy that is available here for initiating new ventures creatively. Instead of wasting it, we must pour it into worthwhile projects. Saturn supports us in this by contributing circumspection and control. If we also keep our awareness and spontaneity, we will be able to act out of an inner certitude, and our actions will be appropriate to the moment. Awareness and spontaneity do not mutually exclude each other. Action is effective when it is based in our gut feeling, and when we are aware and circumspect at the same time.

If we are on a spiritual path, we are striving to dis-identify with the doer, seeing ourself instead as a channel for the creativity of the life-spirit working through us. Cultivating this attitude distances us from our ego, and blesses our doing with a quality of relaxation. We then discover that we are even more productive when we are relaxed, and our openness to what may happen allows more fresh energy to flow into us from the source of life.

Thus the first step on our spiritual journey round the wheel of the houses involves releasing the power within, and learning to express it creatively. When Hercules tamed the wild mares and drove them home to King Eurystheus, he demonstrated his mastery of the untrammelled life-force. He could break them in and harness their energy without breaking their spirit. Then, instead of representing wanton destructiveness, the mares came to symbolise the divine power available to everyone.

The Second House

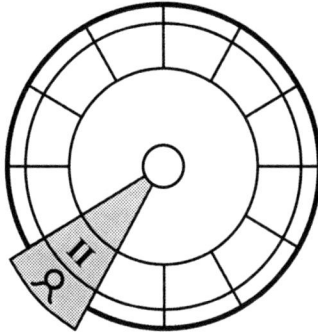

Capturing the Cretan Bull

On the isle of Crete King Minos had built a vast maze wherein he kept a giant bull. Hercules was sent to capture it and bring it back to King Eurystheus. He crossed the sea to Crete and found the labyrinth. For hours he chased the bull through its dark passages, led by the gleaming star on its forehead. At last he captured it and, mounted on its back, crossed the stormy sea to the mainland. Thus he saved the bull's life, as Minos was intending to sacrifice it. And after the bull had been honoured by the people it was set free.

The Earthly Paradise

Moving out of the first into the second house brings a change in the weather. In the first house the climate was rough and raw, like a typical March or early April day in our latitudes, when on venturing out we are buffeted by icy squalls and lashed by showers of sleet. This rowdy, bracing weather soon calms down when the sun enters Taurus. Then warm rays of sunshine penetrate deep into the earth, coaxing the seeds to sprout and the buds to open, and suddenly all the trees are in blossom.

Remnants of the legendary earthly paradise can still be found clustering round the archetype of Taurus and the second house. According to myth it was a time of everlasting spring, when gentle zephyrs caressed the banks of fragrant flowers, rivers flowed with milk and nectar, and golden honey dripped from the green holm oak. It is still there for our taking. In the Beltane month of May, mother earth offers up her bounty for our delight. But are our eyes open to see it, and are we able to receive her gifts?

As the cardinal energy of the first house gives way to fixed, a new phase begins in which what has been initiated is consolidated. And Venus, the second-house ruler, is at hand to help. Her role is to give form and substance to the incentives provided by her partner Mars.[1] As we move round the inner wheel of the horoscope, and yin houses follow yang like an alternating current, this process of expansion followed by contraction is repeated (Fig. 10).

If we have performed our first-house labour well, and have learned to assert ourself and be self-seeking in a positive sense, we can now afford to be gentle and loving. We know that, if it really matters, we can get what we want. But if we held back in the first, and missed the experience of making a supreme effort and being total in

1 See table in Appendix II

our energy, we will be incapable now of letting go and relaxing. So we will be unable to enjoy the fruits of our labours.

Also, if we never learned to get tough with others and set them limits, we will be helpless at protecting our space from those who now try to invade it. In other words, the skills we acquire in the houses we pass through are like credit on our account that we will need to draw on for future investment. 'First things first' is a golden rule as we journey round the wheel, because the labours required of us at each stage build on strengths we should have developed in the houses that went before.

Fig. 10 Yin and Yang Houses

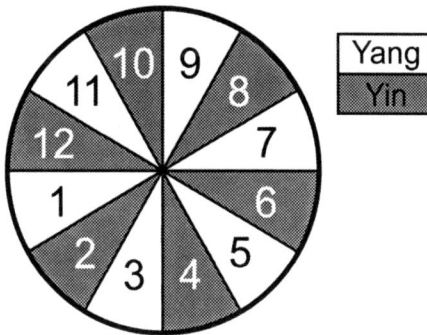

Grounded on the Tarmac - Enjoying the Daisies

The second house cusp forms the first point of the earth trine in the wheel of the houses (Fig. 11). The triangle is a basic figure in sacred geometry[2] and seen as the most stable, because the sum of its internal angles always adds up to 180 degrees or half a circle. Of the four triangles contained in the geometry of the zodiac, the earth triangle, or trine, is the most fixed - earth being the densest and most immobile element.

Fig. 11   The Earth Trine

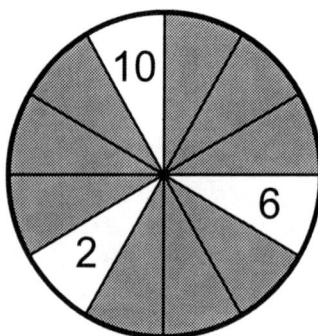

In astrology earth stands as a symbol for material things in all their structural variety. However, quantum physics has proved that the solidity of matter is an illusion.

---

2 The mathematical ideas in the universal mind that manifest as the structural patterning of space and time.

Its ground lies in the volatile quantum flow of waves and particles out of which all forms emerge. The unfolded forms that manifest as thoughts or images in collective and individual minds are shortlived, whereas those that manifest on the material plane endure longer. But at some point even a million-year-old mountain, or a galaxy with a life span of billions of years, will enfold back into the quantum flow again. Nothing material lasts.

But, seen through human eyes, material objects are real and can be relied on. And nowhere is the belief in their reality so strong as in the second house, which also forms the first corner of the fixed cross (Fig. 12). In the fixed houses we try to control things by fixing them, and in fixed earth we do this on the material plane. We seek

Fig. 12 The Fixed Cross

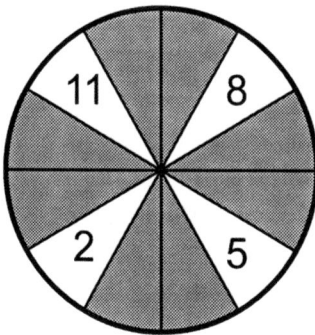

security here through aquiring, holding and maintaining material possessions, and to feel safe we need to put down roots. Therefore at this stage on our journey round the wheel we are banned from flying. Grounded on the tarmac, we have the space to create a stable material foundation on which to build our life - and time to enjoy the daisies!

Life in the Comfort Zone

If you have a second-house sun, whatever sign it is in you will have a side that is like a Taurus. You will tend to fall in love with things - with a house, a car, a suit of fine clothes or some expensive jewellery - and want to own them. You are likely to buy property, and may acquire land or inherit a farm. A nature lover and a conservative committed to preserving traditions, you can become very attached to your favourite stretch of countryside, where you walk your dog every day, always taking the same path. These places, and these material objects, feel like extensions of your own body.

Whether you have too much or too little of it, money will always be an issue in your life. Problems around earning it, spending it and investing it are likely to preoccupy your thoughts and haunt your conversation. However, this one-sidedness is necessary in the second house, where we are learning the value of money, and developing the skills needed to manage it wisely.

With Venus as your house ruler, beauty will be high on your list of values. You may have a talent for beautifying your surroundings, and for looking your handsome best.

You can rely on your aesthetic taste when you choose a hairstyle or some curtains, and you wear your good-quality clothes elegantly. Also, if you are into beauty in a less frivolous way, you may become an artist and enrich the world with beautiful objects of art.

Your physical well-being has high priority, and you heartily dislike leaving your comfort zone. You live through your physical senses, being especially alive to sensations of taste, smell and touch. With such well-developed body-awareness your sensuality level is notched up high. Also you are unashamedly self-indugent, and into enjoying all the pleasures of the flesh - good food, good drink and good sex included.

The Estranged Body

If there are no contra indications in your chart, this is likely to describe you as a second-house person. But it is all turned around when Saturn is in the second. Then our capacity for sensual pleasure can be reduced to the extent that we become sensually numb. And, rather than over-gratifying our physical desires, we will deny that we have them. As if to make the statement that self-indulgence is immoral, our eating and drinking habits could reflect a puritanical asceticism, and we may be reluctant to enjoy sexual pleasure.

Behind these strictures lies an ingrained dislike and mistrust of the body. We may see it as not very nice, even sinful, and so withdraw our awareness from it and retire into our mind. This desensitises our body, causing it to lose its aliveness and become wooden and clumsy.

In contrast, a body that is valued and cared for stays vibrant with life and is graceful. It is not that Saturn in the second house causes us to reject the body. It is rather that he brings body-negating attitudes we are already carrying to our attention, forcing us to confront the fears lying behind them.

Repressed negativity towards the body can also express in the opposite way, and then we become body-obsessed. We are fixated on what we see as our body's faults - for example that our nose is too big or we are too fat. This latter belief can cause eating disorders, or we become addicted to dieting or working-out. On the other hand, if we are obsessed with creating the perfect face and figure, we could spend a fortune on plastic surgery, trying to improve our defects and eradicate all signs of ageing.

Our body-image could be an irrational fixed idea, with no relation to the way we really look. However, our inner negativity is likely to attract negativity from without, which will then serve to fortify our beliefs. For example we may have a mother who keeps criticising how we look and what we wear, or we are married to a partner who keeps complaining that we have put on weight, and says our wrinkles make us look old.

Other people reflect what deep down we believe about ourself. So, if we are on the receiving end of such criticism, it points to us carrying a negative body-image. However, this can be turned round, and a good time to do it is when Saturn is transiting our second house, because then the problems we have with our body will come to a head.

For example, we may notice that our partner is taking an interest in someone younger and prettier, and fear an affair is brewing. We compare ourself to this sexually attractive rival, and find our looks vastly inferior. So we come to the conclusion that there is nothing else for it, to save our relationship we'll have to improve our performance in bed. This idea, however, arouses deep fears. We know full well we are sexually inhibited and have inherited all our parents' hang-ups. There was so much shame and embarrasment around the subject of sex in our family. Is that why we can only make love with the light off?

Our second-house labour is then clear - it involves removing the blocks that have been preventing us from accepting and enjoying our body. There are many therapies, workshops and self-help books around that can give assistance. We can take our pick, but our first step must be to learn to respect our body enough to listen to it. When we no longer see it as an alien, but our body has become a friend, fear and mistrust will turn into appreciation and gratitude.

The Cretan bull is a symbol of the rich fertility of physical life. King Minos, who must have had a body-negating attitude, imprisoned him in a labyrinth of repressed fears and inhibitions, and intended to sacrifice him. But Hercules came to his rescue. Crossing the stormy sea on the way home, mounted on the bull's broad back, he was in touch through his thighs with the full physical power of the animal. So this story, with its happy ending - as the bull is honoured and set free - can be read as an allegory for the healing of our body-negating and sex-negating attitudes.

The Fear of Loss is Worse than Loss

As we have seen, our labour in the second house involves creating a secure material foundation with which to ground ourself on the plane of matter. We need to engage with this plane, and take full possession of our physical body, while we are incarnated here on earth. Saturn will test how well we are doing in this task when he arrives in the second house by transit, and it is then that any cracks and fissures will begin to show. For example, our credit card bill arrives and we get a shock. It seems we have slipped seriously into debt. Then Saturn's transit coincides with a crisis in payments, when we are forced to wake up to the reality of our financial position, and realise the importance of balancing income and expenditure.

Or, if we have been rash and bought a luxurious flat, saddling ourself with a huge mortgage, interest rates could now go shooting up. We realise then that we have over-stretched ourself, and must either downscale or sell up. This kind of decision is particularly stressful in the second house, where downscaling is seen as an invasion of our comfort zone, and we become so attached to our property that we are very loathe to surrender it. But Saturn is pressurising us.

Before we can decide what to dispense with, we must establish our priorities, and this involves defining our needs - which are not necessarily the same as our desires. We must ask ourself what we require materially for our basic well-being. Then everything else that we have or want can be classed as a luxury and not strictly necessary. This is one of the basic distinctions that we need to be clear about in the second house, as our foundation will not firm up until our needs have been clarified and provided for.

One thing is certain - Saturn in the second house intends to make us stand on our own feet financially, so we need not expect material support from others. If we have had a benefactor, when Saturn is transiting the second, his support is likely to be withdrawn. After the initial shock, this could turn out to be a blessing because, when we have proved that we can provide for ourself, it will give a great boost to our self-esteem.

Once we have staked out our territory, we will defend it fiercely in the second house. The fixed energy of the archetype here leads us to try to hold on to what we have acquired. But, looking deeper, we will discover that behind our clinging lies a fear of loss, which insurance companies know how to exploit. Still, however well insured we are, we can never be a hundred percent secure. Something untoward could always happen - like the stock market crashing so we lose our savings, or a natural catastrophe could destroy the home we have invested in. Therefore no peace of mind can be found down this road.

But Saturn, our wise teacher, makes us suffer loss in order to prove to us that we can survive it. And, once we have come through such an experience, we will discover that our fear of loss was worse than the loss itself. Also, the experience of surviving loss serves to strengthen our trust in life, and teaches us to seek our security within ourself. Our second-house labour in this respect is to learn detachment in the Buddhist sense. Buddha taught that attachment to material objects inevitably brings misery, because we are clinging to what we are destined to lose. And in the final instance death will take all - our body included.

To Have and To Be

A second-house Saturn can be a significator for a miser. If we are reluctant to spend money, and if we are hoarders who never throw anything away, we could be reacting to a repressed fear of being poor and destitute. Perhaps we have experienced want in a past life. We may have been forced to scrape a living at subsistence level - perhaps we even starved - in which case it is natural that we unconsciously try to prevent this happening to us again.

So we work hard and earn more and more, and at the same time we scrimp and save so our savings grow and grow, and still it is not enough. However much we have in the bank, we still feel insecure. Then a Saturn transit through our second house could trigger an event that confronts us with the truth about ourself in this respect. And we realise that, although we have all that money, we are incapable of enjoying it. We have become so stingy that we cannot use our money to give ourself and those close to us any pleasure.

To change a deeply ingrained pattern takes work and effort, but Saturn in the second can give us the required determination and consistency. So this could be the time to do some self-development work and inquire into the root of our miserliness. The way forward will be to do therapy together with practising a form of meditation that increases our awareness in day-to-day living.

Another manifestation of a second-house Saturn is the 'poor-me' poor person who wants to attract abundance but so far has failed. If deep down we believe we do not deserve to have money, it will not come our way. So our problem has to do with how we value ourself. Once again there are many workshops and self-help books on this subject that promise to replace our negative mindset with positive beliefs and expectations. And, as our beliefs create our reality, changing them can, at least theoretically, lead to abundance.

In the second house we must examine our core values - the big one being how we value ourself. If we valued ourself, we would give ourself what we need, so is this happening? Or do we secretly think so little of ourself that we need status symbols like a big house and a flashy car to compensate? "To have more is not necessarily to be more", says Saturn, and goes on to prove this by callously removing the material props we relied on to support our ego.

So central to our second-house labour is the healing of our self-esteem. And when this is done and we are able to trust in our inner resources, we can relax at last and begin to live more richly and more generously. We see that existence is showering us every moment with blessings, that there is abundance on every side, and that the best things in life are free.

The Third House

Gathering the Golden Apples
of the Hesperides

Commanded by King Eurystheus to fetch the renowned golden apples of the Hesperides, Hercules set out to search for the garden where they grew. First he had to find the sea-god, Nereus, who was said to know its location. Catching hold of him, Hercules tried to make him tell what he knew. Nereus sought to escape by changing his shape, but Hercules clung on till he had wrested the information from him. His path then led past the rock where Prometheus lay chained. Every day an eagle flew down and pecked at his liver, which afterwards grew back again. Hercules killed the eagle and liberated Prometheus, who in gratitude suggested sending Atlas to fetch the apples. Atlas hated his task of holding up the sky, and would agree just to get rid of it. So Hercules took his place, carrying the weight of the sky on his shoulders, while Atlas departed on his errand. He soon returned with the apples,

43

but then Atlas refused to take back his load. Hercules begged him to shoulder it just for a minute while he put on some padding, and Atlas fell for the ruse. He took back the burden and immediately Hercules, seizing the golden apples, ran off with them.

On the Move

If you were feeling stuck in the fixed earth of the second house and need a change of scenery, you will be glad to hear that things are starting to move now. Crossing into the third house is like entering a wide, open space. The air is fresher, and we feel we can breathe. We also feel lighter as we move forward, buffeted by breezes coming from every side. No wonder it is windy here - we are at the first corner of the air trine in the wheel of the houses (Fig. 13).

Fig. 13   The Air Trine

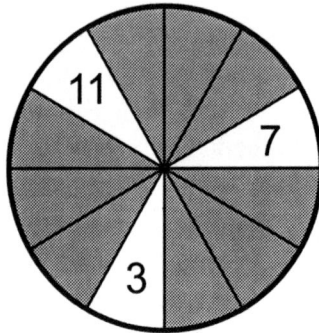

And no wonder the wind keeps changing direction - we are at the first point of the mutable cross (Fig. 14).

Fig. 14   The Mutable Cross

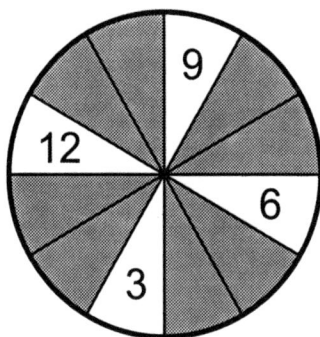

Our house ruler, who is none other than swift Mercury, messenger to the gods, flies along beside us. He is a quintessence of the energy of the Gemini and third-house archetype. In the form of volatile quicksilver his power was invoked by the alchemists of old to destabilise the structure of matter. That makes sense, because something similar is happening now. The mutable air of the third house has started to loosen and dissolve the fixed earth of the second, and is opening everything up.

Many of those medieval alchemists who knew the secret of Mercury's efficacy were travelling scholars, and roamed through Europe on their quest for occult knowledge. Mercury, traditionally also the patron of travellers, watched over them on their journeying. Like the alchemists, or like Hercules, we are on a quest for knowledge in the third house. Hercules wandered about for quite a while before he found Nereus, and was able to obtain from him the information he sought.

A Butterfly Tasting Pollen

When your sun is in the third house, whatever sign it is in you will have an airy and mercurial side that is like a Gemini. There will be something childlike about you - something carefree that does not take life seriously. Charming, clever and amusing, you will be able to talk about any subject that comes into your head and make it sound interesting.

You are found out in the world where there's plenty happening. Driven by your curiosity and by a dread of boredom, you make sure your mind receives enough mental stimuli. The element air, which in the macrocosm lies over the planes of earth and water, corresponds in the microcosm to the mind, which is above and beyond the body and emotions. This may explain why you live in your head, and like to adopt an aloof, objective stance, detached from your feelings. You believe you are your mind, just as a second-house person believes he is his body.

Reason is your guiding light, and rationality is what you aspire and appeal to. You may be one of those intellectuals who learns to juggle abstract concepts, and creates an academic career through this skill. Or you may be a research worker or a journalist, involved in collecting or disseminating information. Your lively mind is flexible and open to new ideas, so you are ready to accomodate other people's opinions, and often to adopt them as your own.

A sun in the third house usually implies gregariousness, so you are likely to know a lot of people. These will not be friends in the close sense, but rather a loose network of acquaintances. In the past you would write them letters. Today you stay in contact via email and your mobile phone. However, as you keep on the move, a lack of commitment could be evident in your relationships. And, until you are caught, and more or less forcibly led to the altar, you will try to keep all your options open.

As the Gemini archetype is dual in nature, a third-house person can have a split personality, so there may be two distinct sides to you. Each side has different ideas and different needs, so you will often feel divided. Then, in situations where you have to make a choice between them, you will try to have it both ways, which is why you keep tying yourself in knots!

One advantage to having more than one string to your bow is that you will be good at multi-tasking. So we often find you doing several things at once. You may even lead a double life - dividing yourself between two jobs, two homes or two families, as you try to explore all the avenues open to you. However, living in this way results in life experience that may be broadly based but is also shallow.

Similarly, although you are multi-talented, and can turn your hand to many different trades, you are likely to be master of none, because you lack sticking power. So you will take things up, only to lose interest and drop them again. With a third-house sun, unless there are contra indications, you are happiest fluttering like a butterfly over the surface of life, tasting the pollen here and there and moving on. Surfing is the modern word for it.

Saturn Concentrates the Mind

Our labour in the third house is to sharpen our perception and improve our mind. We are making of it an efficient tool for comprehending the world, and managing our personal life. And the more we know about the world about us, the more secure we will feel. Knowledge is power - or so we believe. Therefore we are out to discover the facts, and to accumulate a body of knowledge we can rely on. This is not as easy as it sounds, because first we have to get the facts straight, and the truth often turns out to be more subtle than our rational mind can conceive.

Having Saturn in the third house in our birth chart is helpful here, as Saturn concentrates the mind. Wherever he is found, he brings with him the qualities of the Capricorn archetype. These will have a stabilising effect on the shifting field of mutable air. So in the third house Saturn can contribute qualities of rigour, thoroughness and consistency to any form of mental work.

However there is a downside. A dose of the Capricorn archetype has the effect of suppressing the playful and ebullient third-house energy and making it heavy, which results in a pessimistic or even cynical attitude to life. So we are likely to become very serious, and also hyper-critical, tending to see faults rather than virtues and to judge them harshly. Behind our strictures could lie an intellectual inferiority complex, which can be very debilitating as far as our mental ambitions are concerned.

When Saturn is not in the third natally, but enters this house in transit, he could pull us up sharp. If we have been muddling along in a happy-go-lucky way, we will find this no longer suffices to deal with the situations now arising. For example, vital information could go missing at work and we get the blame, putting the job we love at risk. Or we muddle our schedule and double-book ourself, which leads to us missing an important appointment on which much hangs. Or a verbal misunderstanding results in a relationship being broken off just when we relied on it - little things can have big repercussions.

This adverse experience means Saturn is teaching us to concentrate our mind. We must learn to be all there, totally present and alert, so no important detail is missed. In other words it is time to notch up our awareness one peg higher. During a Saturn transit we will find it hard to evade issues by using the usual escape routes, because he will find ways to nail us down. So we should see his transit positively. It is our chance to acquire some character strengths we may have lacked - for example self-discipline, stamina and sticking power. Also, if we were in the habit of talking too much, and in a long-winded way, Saturn in the third will exhort us to express ourself briefly and succinctly. He will make us realise how important it is to stay aware of what we are saying and why we are saying it.

Some people use a Saturn transit through the third to begin a course of study that will improve their qualifications and career propects. Others take an exam, finish their thesis, or get their book written at last, as it is a good time for a sustained intellectual effort. But, when we finally settle down to it, we may discover that, although we know a little about a lot, we lack the in-depth knowledge now required of us. So there is nothing for it. We have to knuckle down and acquire it.

If we perform our labour properly, this period in our lives can result in achievements we are later proud of, which boost our confidence in our intelligence and fortify our self-esteem. In other words we have managed to find Nereus, to kill the eagle, to free Prometheus, to carry the sky on our shoulders and now, finally, the golden apples are within reach - and all that within the space of two and a half years, the duration of a Saturn transit through the third house!

I Think Therefore I Am

Our third-house labour is an important step in our individuation process. Through learning to think for ourself, and to use our brain, we develop our mental body. We also strengthen our sense of personal identity. In this house to know what we think is to know who we are. However, if we live in the mind only, we are in danger of losing our grounding. It is our body and our emotions that give us a coherent and consistent sense of self and, if we lose touch with them, we are like a kite that has lost its string.

'Cogito ergo sum' - I think therefore I am. If we believe this is the case, then it proves we are identified with our minds. We could then fear that if we stop thinking or talking we stop existing. Perhaps this is why some third-house people go on yackety-yacking all the time, compulsively verbalising whatever comes into their head, relevant or irrelevant.

Behind our third-house quest for ever-new information lies a need to find the ideas we can identify with. For this reason we expose ourself daily to a steady flow of information from the media, devour a copious amount of printed matter, and glean the latest local news from gossip sessions with our friends. Much of it goes in one ear and out the other, but some ideas stick.

Part of the process of testing ideas to find ones we agree with involves trying out concepts on others. So we may expound on ideas that we have only partly digested to see how people react to them. For this reason our opinions on various subjects may be temporary, and are not to be relied on. In the third house we often change our minds about what we believe. But finally, after much mental threshing and winnowing, we are left with a set of opinions that we can call our own.

Thick as a Plank

When natal Saturn is in the third, we could have an intellectual inferiority complex and be unconsciously trying to compensate for it. So, for example, if we notice ourself talking a lot in order to draw attention to ourself, and trying impress others with how much we know, this could be because we are bolstering our ego by proving we are intelligent after all. Or we could be very quiet and never say a thing, for fear of betraying that we are stupid.

Complexes like these could stem from our past lives. Perhaps we were denied an education in our last life because of our social rank. Perhaps we had learning difficulties or some mental handicap, and acquired a reputation for being thick. If we internalised this, it could be still present as a belief somewhere in our unconscious. How we see ourself inside is always reflected in how we are seen by others. So we are caught in a vicious circle, in which the opinion of our parents and our teachers that we are not very bright only serves to deepen our inferiority complex still further.

Saturn in the third natally can also indicate that we were disadvantaged educationally in our childhood through our parents moving home a lot. This meant we had to keep making new starts at new schools and lost ground. If this was the case, we were often put in the position of an outsider, wanting to be accepted by the group but feeling alienated. Such an experience also leaves its mark, and later in life we could feel awkward and out of place in company, expecting people not to like or accept us.

We may compensate for these hang-ups by studying obsessively. There are people who read the encyclopaedia page by page, attempting to learn its contents. They acquire general knowledge of TV gameshow standard, without asking themselves what use it is to them. Others strive for high academic qualifications, which impress others, to reassure themselves that they are clever after all.

Some compensate for their social inferiority complex by spending every evening in the pub, trying to be popular and proving they belong.

When Saturn passes through the third in transit, problems like these, which we may have ignored, are exacerbated by our circumstances. These bring us into situations in which our traumas can be relived. Thus Saturn pushes us to investigate the cause of our inhibitions. If this transit happens in old age, and our ego pride has rested on what and who we know, Saturn could have a cruel hubris in store for us. We may lose our memory and end up isolated and demented - an experience some may need in order to let go of their mind and enter the plane of pure consciousness.

This fate is only for a minority. In every case, however, as we grow older we find that the world has moved on, and the things we thought we knew for a fact have been disproved. Human knowledge, we must learn, is a transient, insubstantial thing, and in the final instance Socrates was right when he said that the only thing we can know for sure is that we know nothing.

The Golden Apples of the Hesperides

The golden apples growing on the tree of knowledge in the garden of the Hesperides symbolise wisdom. As such they represent the prize to be won at the end of the journey during which our understanding is deepened, and our awareness is sharpened. They were gathered in the story by Atlas, who was a bit thick and could not recognise their value. Then Hercules, who was brighter, used his wits to out-trick Atlas and so came by them. But they were not his rightful possession either, and he had to deliver them up to the king.

The apples also stand for the right use of our mental powers. We become the master of our mind through avoiding becoming identified with it. We discover that, although the ego can be bolstered by knowledge, the being can not. So to know more is not necessarily to be more. And we also discover that, when we are identified with the mind, this prevents us from experiencing greater dimensions of reality.

Meditation can give us the experience of stepping out of the mind and into the being. Through learning the art of witnessing our thoughts, we detach ourself from them, and come to know experientially that we are not our mind - we are consciousness. As we move deeper into meditation, and our outer talking becomes less, our inner chatter also subsides, and we discover the bliss of silence. So we may enter the dimension of consciousness beyond the mind, which is the dimension of divine wisdom and eternal being.

The Fourth House

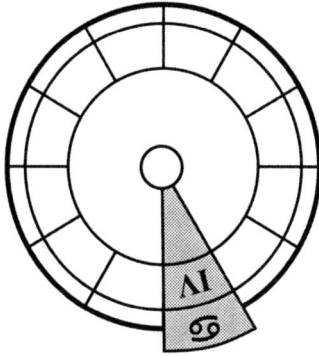

Capturing the Doe with the Golden Antlers

Two goddesses, Diana and Artemis, were quarrelling over the possession of a doe. Artemis claimed it was hers because she had tended it when young. Diana said it belonged to her now, and refused to give it up. So Hercules was sent to capture the doe, and bring her to Eurystheus who would decide the question. For a whole year he followed her tracks, and at last surprised her while she was crossing a stream. He shot an arrow in her leg which lamed her, making her easy to seize. Then he slung her over his shoulders and carried her away. But Diana furiously intercepted him, and accused him of trying to kill her sacred animal. Hercules replied, "The doe is now mine by right of my skill and the prowess of my arm." Then he explained how he must perform this labour as part of his penance. When Diana heard his story, her anger turned to pity. She healed the doe's wound and allowed Hercules to carry it to Eurystheus, who immediately set it free.

In Deep Water

Although we learned a lot in the third house, learning to feel was not on our agenda there. We were deep in thought and thinking precludes feeling, so this must now be rectified. Our labour in the fourth house will be to balance the power of the mind with the power of the feeling heart. In the myth the heart is represented by the gentle doe, so shy and so vulnerable.

When we enter the fourth house, we have reached the nadir of the inner wheel. The sun on its diurnal round passes this point at midnight when most of us are deep asleep. Consequently the fourth house represents the darkest, in the sense of the most unconscious, part of ourself. The world outside, that held our attention in the third house, loses its attraction now, and our focus of interest turns inwards to our private sphere and our inner life.

Falling asleep is like diving to the bottom of the sea. We leave our surface consciousness and sink through the shallow waters of the dream state, where weird and wonderful sea creatures appear and disappear, to finally rest on the seabed in the oblivion of the deep sleep phase. The metaphor is apt as the fourth house symbolises among other things the primeval ocean out of which all life emerged, and the salt water of the womb where our personal life began as an embryo. It represents both the origins of our life and its end - as we are going to end where we began.

We have arrived at the first point of the water trine in the inner wheel (Fig. 15), and water symbolises our emotional body. It includes our feelings and our psyche that flows on a deep level into the collective unconscious. In the fourth house our personal unconscious meets and merges with that of our family. Here the energy lines of our family tree run backwards through time from our parents to the ancestors whose genes we carry, branching out ever more until they include the whole race.

Fig. 15   The Water Trine

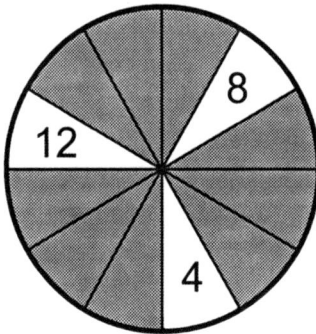

So, if we are unavailable in the fourth, it is because our attention is being drawn down into our inner water. We need to submerge regularly as there is work to be done down there. It involves revisiting our past in order to heal and refine our emotional body. At this stage on our evolutionary path, we must make our psychosomatic foundations stable enough to give us emotional security, and support our sense of self.

It is no coincidence that Diana claimed the doe as her sacred animal, as she is goddess of the moon as well as of the hunt. In the fourth house we come under the influence of the moon as our house ruler. In the macrocosm she governs the ebb and flow of the tides, and in the microcosm the flow of fluids through the body. She is associated with women in their capacity to gestate and bring forth, and rules pregnancy, birth and the female fertility cycle. So we can expect to confront our emotional and irrational female side in the fourth house, and women's issues in some form could be on our agenda.

We have also reached the second corner of the cardinal cross (Fig. 9, page 19) where a new quadrant begins (Fig. 6, page 12). In our journey round the wheel, each time we reach an angular house there is an influx of fresh energy to carry us onward, and when we enter a new quadrant a new level of meaning opens up.

In the quadrants below the horizon the focus is on our individuation process. In the first quadrant, that now lies behind us, we have been reconditioning our sense of self, and creating a new identity. In the second quadrant this work will continue, but our growth opportunities will come increasingly through our relationships. The quadrants represent an evolutionary path in themselves, as each has a different emphasis and builds on the skills developed in the preceding ones.

The Crab Archetype

If our sun is in the fourth, we will have a side like a Cancer that will express the crab archetype. So, unless there are contra indications, we are going to view life through the glass of our subjective feelings, and judge according to our personal likes and dislikes. When we are in an introverted mood, we will want to be left alone. Then we can be grouchy and react over-sensitively if disturbed. Others will come up against the hardness of our shell and feel our steely claws, but we only put them out in self-defence. At other times we are welcoming, and bathe our loved-ones in a pool of warm, cosy intimacy.

With a fourth-house sun, our life is likely to revolve round our family. If we have children, we'll be busy nurturing them, and if we don't, we'll find child replacements in partners, pets or patients. We are protective and caring towards those we love and always ready to give emotional support. But we expect something in return. When we are feeling weak and needy ourself - which can be quite often - we'll expect the family to rally round. And, if they don't, we can turn resentful and feel very sorry for ourself.

We express the active energy of this cardinal field through keeping ourself busy all the time. But water is also a passive, introverted element, so, while we are busying about, we are also dreaming. Our attention is focused on our inner life rather than on what we are doing, as the continuous flow of feelings, memories and imaginings passing through us seems more real than the outer world. Our water also gives us empathy and heightens our intuition, so we sense the feelings and desires of those close to us, and know instinctively what they need.

Owning our house or flat will be important to us in the fourth, which is traditionally the house of landed property. We need our own private space where outsiders do not intrude, and where we feel safe. We will use our creativity to make it into a warm, comfortable home, where the whole family like to congregate and enjoy our home cooking. We may be still living in the family home where we grew up, as we never like to stray far from our roots in the fourth and get emotionally attached to their locality.

If there are no contra indications, a sun in the fourth will indicate that we enjoyed a happy and secure childhood in the bosom of a loving family. We will have a strong bond with our mother and tend to identify with her. We will often dwell nostalgically on the past, and be sentimental about old keepsakes and momentos. Perhaps we will take an interest in local history, and collect old photographs or other remanants of byegone days.

The Dysfunctional Family

This is all turned round when natal Saturn is in our fourth house. Then we will also dwell on the past, but our memories are likely to be unhappy ones. Saturn in this placement indicates that we grew up in an emotionally cold home, which we remember later as a place of oppression and limitation. Perhaps we were a lonely only child, or perhaps both our parents worked and had no time for us, or perhaps our mother suffered from depression or some other emotional disorder, and was unable to give us love and care. We may have been cruelly treated - beaten or abused - and then spend the rest of our life dealing with the aftermath.

We will go on repeating our patterns until we change them. So, when we create a family of our own, it is also likely to be dysfunctional. Our outer environment will reflect our inner disharmony, and our family life will be full of emotional turmoil. At some point, however, we may have had enough, and then we could turn to therapy to solve our problems which we will see as originating in our childhood. In this case we must beware of casting ourself in the role of victim. If we see our parents as the baddies, and ourself as their helpless victim, we will be full of blame - an attitude that brings us to a full stop on our evolutionary path, as the past cannot be undone.

Yet, although the past cannot be changed, we can change how we see it. Then, in order to move on, our first step will be to accept what happened and take some responsibility for it. For example, we can see our unfair start in this life as karma we had to pay. In the context of past lives it is conceivable that we once also neglected our children or treated a child cruelly, in which case we needed to experience similar suffering to theirs. In this way we come to understand the harm we did, and our heart is softened.

With Saturn in the fourth we may have been abandonned by our parents in early childhood - dumped in a boarding school at a tender age, for example, or farmed out to foster parents. Or our parents could have split up, so we lost the father or mother we loved and gained a step-parent instead who persecuted us. We can react to this sort of experience in different ways. The first is to close our heart to make sure it does not get wounded again. Then we learn to keep aloof from our feelings, and later in life we avoid close emotional relationships and are incapable of intimacy.

The second is the way of compensation where we go to the other extreme. We forge tight emotional bonds with our partners and children to keep them in our power and prevent them from ever leaving us. Deep down we believe we could not survive without them, and that we need them for our emotional security. Thus co-dependent relationships form that prevent us from maturing and becoming independent. And we can remain stuck in this pattern for a long time too.

The Home Front

During a Saturn transit through the fourth house, family relationships can become so fraught that they spark off a major crisis. It's Saturn again, putting us under pressure to take the next step. This could be the time when the emotional turbulence at home starts making us ill. Or a partner or child could break away from us in spite of our attempts to hold them. Bonds that are too constricting and that limit our personal growth must now be severed.

So the worst could happen - the thing we always feared most - and we are left alone. The house feels like a cold and empty place now and, thrown back on ourself after so many years of being preoccupied with others and their needs, we do not know how to fill our time. Saturn has no compunction about thowing us into the deep end and leaving us to sink or swim.

If we sink we become resentful and self-pitying, and we may try to manipulate the feelings of the person who has left us to make them feel guilty in the hope they will return. We stew in our misery, and our negative feelings weigh us down, so we are too heavy to progress on our evolutionary path.

A separation from a loved-one is a hard test - even the goddess Diana found it hard to lose her doe. She could not bring herself to give it up and clung to it fiercely. So she was furious when Hercules came to take it away. But his action brought things to a head and, although Diana was angry at first, a deeper understanding of the situation opened her heart and she become compassionate. So she healed the doe's wound, thus healing the emotional wound in her own heart caused by the rift with her sister, Artemis.

A Saturn transit in the fourth can express in many ways that are all geared to making us emotionally more mature. It will force us to inquire into ourself, and investigate the deeper emotional problems disturbing our inner harmony. And we will not be able to let go of our outer props, and find happiness and security within ourself, until our emotional foundations have been stabilised.

For example, an aged parent becomes in need of care, meaning extra work and responsibility. We decide to adapt our house to accomodate him or her, and get the builders in. But then a long and wearisome saga begins during which the builders, who prove unreliable, make slow progress, and finally leave the job unfinished. In this case we should ask ourself whether we really want the aged parent to live with us at all. Perhaps these difficult outer circumstances are reflecting our inner resistance to the idea.

Further self-inquiry then makes us realise that we still have some inner work to do. Emotional wounds, deriving from our past relationship with this parent, need to be healed. In other words it is no use trying to refurbish our house, unless at the same time we recondition our emotional body. Whatever our story, when Saturn is in the fourth it is crucial to revisit our past and finish any unfinished family business, or else the repressed feelings that we have not yet dealt with will erupt on our home front, and disturb the happy, harmonious family life we were trying to create.

Becoming the Master of Emotion

The healing work of the fourth house involves deepening our general psychological understanding. When we understand ourself and our loved-ones better, it helps us drop the negative feelings towards them we were carrying, and we become more compassionate and forgiving. Astrology with its explanatory power can help us here, but we have other options. We may find a psychotherapist who takes us through our childhood and uncovers the root of our problems. We may do primal therapy or family constellation work - both of which help to heal family wounds. We may use self-help books to become our own therapist. All these ways can give us a deeper understanding of our emotional patterns.

In the fourth house, our moods shift and change like the moon. Until we reach a certain level of awareness, we are governed by our instinctive emotional responses, and can become so overwhelmed by our feelings that we lose our higher consciousness with its overview of the situation. When we come to realise that our emotions are running our life, we may decide to put an end to this by becoming their master rather than their slave.

Learning to meditate is the best way of developing mastery of our feelings. In meditation we are aware of the fluctuations in our emotional body from moment to moment, and can watch our emotional patterns. We see, for example, how giving energy to negative feelings through dwelling on them intensifies them, and how, if we repress negative feelings, this drains our energy.

No emotion should be denied, so we must start by accepting the emotional state we are in and, through observing it, try to understand it better. Slowly we come to realise that we can attain a level of consciousness where we have a choice; either we can get lost in negative feelings or we can nourish ourself with positive ones instead.

It is through maintaining this level of awareness, and practising choosing from moment to moment which feelings to feel, that we become the master of our emotions. And once we can change negative feelings into positive ones, our heart that was once so full of neediness transforms into a heart full of love. Then we are no longer in danger of becoming emotionally dependent on others, and we can use our strong feelings as a source of creative power.

After Diana's anger was transformed into love and compassion, she was able to heal the wound to the doe's leg, which was a wound to her heart. So before we can receive love, we must first give it and, before we can give love, we must remove the obstacles that were preventing our heart from opening. The hard feelings that crystallised round our wounds to protect them must melt away before they can heal.

It is fitting that, when Hercules finally delivered up the golden-antlered doe to Eurystheus, the great king set it free. With this gesture he was saying that the doe, symbolising love, belongs to no one person because love is always free and must always be freely given - or else it is not love.

The Fifth House

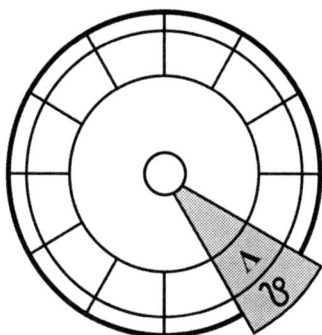

Slaying the Nemean Lion

Hercules arrives to slay the terrible lion who is terrorising the land of Nemea. Taking up his great bow, he shoots all his arrows at it, but they fail to pierce the lion's thick pelt. Then, throwing his bow away, he rushes at the lion bare-handed, who retreats and hides in a cave. Hercules sees that the cave has two openings, and blocks one up. Then he enters through the other and wrestles with it. Finally, summoning all his strength, he strangles the lion with his bare hands. This done he strips off its pelt. Henceforth Hercules always wears the lion skin in battle as it has the magic property of making him invincible.

In the Temple of the Sun

As we emerge from the shadowy depths of the fourth house into the bright light of the fifth, we leave behind the watery realm of the moon and enter the temple of the sun. The sun, ruler of the fifth house and carrier of the Leo archetype, has pride of place at the centre of our solar system, from where it dispenses heat and light to nourish its retinue of planets. In the ancient system of analogies, the sun corresponded to gold - the most valuable of metals. Likewise it corresponded to the king, who was head of state, and to the lion, the king of the animals.

The sun is a star burning out of its own centre, consuming itself while maintaining a steady state, and as such stands as a literal example for fixed fire, the energy quality of the fifth house. Although its fixity is relative, as the sun also has a life cycle, change on such a vast time scale is imperceptible to human senses, so in our eyes the sun stays the same. Its central fixed position guarantees order, ensuring the regularity of the rhythm of day and night, and the round of the seasons that make life on earth viable.

In the fifth house our task will be to find our own fixed centre. We each have an inner sun corresponding to the outer one and, if we can find it and express it, we come into our power. Plugged in to the solar power supply in our core, we tap into a source of cosmic energy that continually recharges our batteries. Then we shine like a bright star, radiating out our heat and light in the form of enthusiasm for life and creative inspiration.

At this second point of the fire trine (Fig. 8, page 18), the flame ignited in the first house flares up more strongly. We need to come out now and show ourself. We know we have a lot to give, and we must find ways of demonstrating our strengths, and making an impact through expressing our unique talents.

The fifth house is also the beginning of the second trigant. We have seen how the wheel of the houses can be divided into four quadrants (Fig. 6, page 12), but we can also divide it into three groups of four houses, which I call trigants (Fig. 7, page 13). On reaching the fifth house, we have passed once through all four elements of the first trigant - fire, earth, air and water. Now, in houses five to eight, we will run through them again in the same sequence, but our experience of them this second time round will be on a different level.

The difference between the first and the second trigants is that in the first we get to know ourself from within, whereas in the second we get to know ourself from without. For example, in the first house we discovered and acted out our personal fire. Now in the fifth the quality of our fire will be tested in our interaction with others. How people react to us and to what we achieve must be taken on board as feedback, and will modify how we see ourself. Thus in the second trigant other people are like mirrors, and we deepen our self-knowledge through experiencing the way they reflect us.

The fifth house is also the second point of the fixed cross (Fig. 12, page 33). As we move from cardinal to fixed energy fields, the strong outward energy thrust is balanced and contained. A time of relative stability begins in which we have space to integrate the experience we gathered in the previous phase of innovation. In this case the emotional power accrued in the fourth house is concentrated in the fifth, where it can be used as a catalyst for creative activity.

In the fifth house we are still in the lower hemisphere of the wheel, where our task is to find ourself as an individual and develop our personal strengths. And in this house of the sun we need to shine - which means coming out and showing the world who we are and what we can do. So we express our talents and then wait for a response, whereby what matters is not what we achieve but that we achieve it. We are exploring creative power as such, but while we do so our self-esteem is at stake. So, when what we have created is appreciated, we feel valued in ourself but, if it is rejected, we will take this as a personal rejection.

In other words our achievements in the fifth serve to boost the ego. However, this is not what we want if we are on a spiritual path. Just the opposite - we want to drop the ego! But we cannot do so until we have grown an ego that is worth dropping, and this is on our fifth-house agenda. It is the place on our evolutionary path where the ego must fatten and ripen, so that later it can drop from the bough like a mature fruit.

Hercules Wearing the Lion Skin

If our natal sun is in the fifth, a part of us will express the Leo archetype, and we will not see ourself as run of the mill. We have been born with special talents, and others should recognise this and give us precedence. We believe we were born to command, and certainly look the part, as our bearing is proud and upright. When we enter a room, people look up and take notice. Perhaps it is our strong belief in ourself that is the secret of our charisma.

In the dramatised story of our life we have cast ourself as the star, and given others supporting roles. But, although we are so full of ourself, and are blatantly attention-seeking, people enjoy our company. We are such fun to be with. Our creative ideas bring a sparkle into people's lives, and the warmth and positivity we radiate attracts them like bears to honey. So we are never short of friends and followers who are more than happy to support us in our endeavours.

Many people who have the sun in the fifth are artists, actors or musicians - professions that allow them to dress and behave in ways that make them stand out from the crowd. A lot of this is bluff and image, but among them are many talented and creative people who are dedicated to their art and produce work of a high standard.

Children and creativity are bracketed together as fifth-house subject matter, and an artist could see the work he has produced with so much hard labour as his child, just as parents could see the child they have borne and laboriously brought up as their work of art. Children are their parents' gift to the world, and raising them is a creatively challenging task, so the two themes have much in common.

Not everyone becomes an artist, but all of us are potential progenitors when we reach puberty, and are empowered by our biology to create new life. And it is the love affairs, also assigned to the fifth, that often lead to procreation - albeit unwanted.

If we have a fifth-house sun, we'll naturally take the lead, and will aspire to a position of power and responsibility. Our pride will not allow us to settle for less than the top job. Thus we are likely to be voted form-captain in our class at school, and become head-girl and later a head-mistress, if we go into teaching, or the head of some other department. People believe in us, and our superiors are impressed by our confident decision-making and our organisational ability. As our pride prevents us from ever admitting we are ill, uncertain, confused or in any way incompetent, we appear invincible. But this is just a front. We are wearing the lion skin which makes us feel strong and hides our weaknesses.

Once we have got the top job and are seated on our throne, it will be hard to dislodge us. In this field of fixed fire we hang on like grim death to a position of power once we have it. So fifth-house people are still found at their posts long after their sell-by date.

If the Sun and Moon Should Doubt

We have the same need to be creative and share our gifts with others when natal Saturn is in our fifth house, but something will be blocking us, and we are likely to hide our light under a bushel. It seems we have come into this life carrying a deep self-doubt, which may be derived from experiences of failure and rejection in a past life. This creates negative expectations in us about our chances of success which then hold us back. William Blake wrote, "If the sun and moon should doubt, they'd immediately go out," vividly expressing how our doubts and fears prevent our inner sun from shining.

If we search for clues in our early life, we may remember occasions when something we had created to the best of our ability was rejected and derided instead of being praised. Or some authority figure kept putting us down, impressing upon us that we were no good and would never come to anything. Perhaps this was so painful, and wounded us so deeply, that we decided to prevent it ever happening again. So we have been hiding behind a wall of defence ever since, careful not to put our head over the top in case it gets shot at.

Therefore, although we may be exceptionally gifted, with Saturn in the fifth we have a block to overcome before we can express our talents. Our expectation is that what we have created will not be valued or appreciated. So we need a lot of encouragement before we try something, and a lot of praise before we finish it, and even then we are cynical about the whole thing. Unfortunately we are also likely to be envious, and therefore critical, of what other people create.

At the root of this pattern lies an ancient past-life-wound to our self-esteem, deepened by experiences of rejection in this present life. The less we believe in ourself, the more we need other people to validate us. This is why, when Saturn is in the fifth, we suffer so acutely when we lose face and are made to look foolish, because the little self-esteem that we have rests on other people's good opinion of us.

Saturn's placement in this house brings qualities of the Capricorn archteype to merge with those of Leo, so our motivation behind our drive for power will be to take and maintain control. In a position of authority we are likely to be autocratic and tyrannical, as we try to compensate for our hidden inferiority complex by dominating and subjugating others. Some people with fifth-house Saturns become bullies, not because they are strong and confident - just the opposite, out of fear of their inner weakness.

In cases such as these, our fifth-house labour involves understanding the roots of our lust for power, and the reason why we abuse power when we have it. Were we dominated and humiliated in our childhood by a parent, a teacher or an older child? If so the experience may have been so traumatic that we made an inner decision to prevent it happening again. And our way of doing so is to ensure that we hold the reins of power.

However, compensating for a shaky self-esteem need not necessarily make a heartless tyrant of us. We could become a celebrity with fans to reassure us that we are loved. But the more limelight we take, the more we will clash with other egos who are trying to do the same, and so we get caught up in power-struggles and rivalries. It is not good to raise our profile by trying to elevate ourself at another's expense - for example through denigrating the work of a fellow artist. Nobility is required of us in the fifth, as to be a true hero we must play fair, and our rivalry with others should be sportsmanlike.

With their heroic feats to make a name, and great achievements to win fame, many history book heroes must have been unconsciously compensating for an inferiority complex. Even Hercules felt inferior. He was ashamed of slaying his wife and children when he was not in his right mind, and his labours, seen in this context, become efforts to restore his belief in himself, and to prove to the world that he was not a malefactor but a hero.

Healing the Self-Esteem

A Saturn transit through the fifth house will put us under pressure to enter the inner cave and wrestle with the beast. When the lion, that was so proud and dominant, has shown itself a coward by running away, it will sit there in the dark brooding. Then a harsh rejection or sharp criticism will be a goad to it, and it will growl and howl and remind us it is there. So, like Hercules, we must enter the cave and take it on. But first we must block up the second entrance, as the lion will escape if it can avoid confrontation. Thus we are brought to face the truth of our inner fears and our deeper feelings of inferiority.

During a Saturn transit in the fifth, we have an opportunity to investigate these feelings, and focus on who we really are rather than on how we want the world to see us. It becomes more important to know our reality than to promote a touched-up image. And, when we have become aware of the fragile shell of our ego, and of the inferiority complex it covers, it becomes our labour to investigate where this complex came from and find a cure for it.

For example, if we have a creative profession, during a Saturn transit in the fifth we could suffer from writer's or artist's block. Then we become so self-critical that we rubbish what we have done so far, and lose our motivation to continue. What triggered this block remains a mystery if we don't know our astrology but, if we do, we could blame it on Saturn bringing out our repressed self-doubt. To make progress on our spiritual path, our relationship with ourself needs to be reconstituted, which involves becoming conscious of our inferiority complex, and how we try to compensate for it. So Saturn is only doing his job.

To take a more extreme example, we could fail in a big way and suffer a public humiliation, so it becomes apparent to all how far short we fall of the superman image we were promoting. When our feeling of self-worth is shaky, losing face is very threatening. It strips us of our outer supports, but the good news is that it will throw us back on ourself and force us to look inside. Saturn is determined to reveal what we are hiding beneath our lion skin.

Or a Saturn transit in the fifth could coincide with some brilliant person coming into our life, who eclipses us by appearing more intelligent, more gifted and more successful than we are. Our self-confidence is so deflated in their presence that we feel like a nobody. If this annoys us, it goes to show that we are making the mistake of using other people as measuring sticks, instead of defining ourself in our own terms.

Comparison, by which we see ourself as either superior or inferior to others, is the main fault in our thinking in the fifth house. The ego is created and maintained through comparison, and would disappear if we were alone on the planet. It is necessary to put the ego aside, and stop judging and comparing, in order to appreciate the uniqueness of each individual. When we can accept both others and ourself as we really are, the ego vanishes like mist at sunrise, whereupon our inner sun immediately shines more brightly and intensely.

Others always mirror the way we experience ourself, so we must recognise ourself before we can be recognised, and love ourself before we are loved. The way forward, if we are to heal our wounded self-esteem, is to give ourself the approval and recognition we were erroneously seeking from others. Then, instead of seeing what is wrong with us, we will see what is right. And through acknowledging our achievements, however small, and praising our successes, we will transform our negative self-image into a positive one.

Self-Mastery

On the evolutionary path it becomes more important to master ourself than to master others, and Hercules' fifth labour can be seen as a metaphor for the process of self-mastery. The lion terrorising the land of Nemea was behaving like someone compensating for an inferiority complex through exercising untrammelled power. It is an example of what happens when an ego is out of control. In wrestling with the beast, Hercules is wrestling with his own lower nature - that part of himself capable of abusing his superhuman strength and becoming a cruel predator.

Hercules defeats the lion in a fair and honest fight without the use of weapons, relying on his innate strength and empowered by his integrity. When it is all over, he appears before the people wearing the lion's pelt that now symbolises, not a facade but the spiritual strengths accrued through passing this hard test. And thenceforth, whenever he wears it, he is protected from harm.

Although he was celebrated by the people of Nemea, Hercules was no longer dependent on their praise. He was not in need of validation now, as he had validated himself. Thus their applause no longer made him feel almighty, just as their rejection would never be able to shatter him. He had found the gold at the centre of his being.

The Sixth House

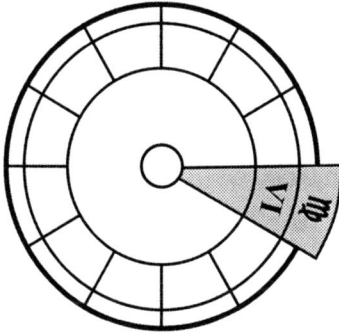

Seizing the Girdle of Hippolyte

Hippolyte, queen of the Amazons, wore a protective girdle that was coveted by Eurystheus' daughter. Hercules was sent to fetch it, and so sailed to the land of the Amazons with a band of men. When Hippolyte heard he was coming she went to meet him, prepared to surrender the girdle. But the rumour spread among her women that Hercules had come to carry off their queen, and so they armed themselves. Thus, when Hercules landed, a battle ensued during which Hercules slew Hippolyte and took the girdle from her.

Arriving at the seashore, he saw a great sea serpent emerge from the waves and seize a young maiden. He rushed to her aid but too late - she disappeared down its throat. The monster then seized Hercules and also swallowed him alive. There within its great belly he found the maiden and was able to carry her out, hacking a passage with his sword. Then, having saved her life, he returned to Eurystheus carrying the girdle.

Harvest Time

In its daily round the sun passes the sixth house in the evening, and reaches the corresponding sign of Virgo at harvest time in its yearly cycle. Imagine a peaceful, late summer scene in the countryside, with the golden sun setting over the stubbled fields, and the swifts weaving patterns in the air as they swoop after flies. The harvesters are still at work, making use of the last hours of daylight. They use a combine-harvester, but in the past they would have loaded the sweet-smelling, freshly-cut corn onto carts to take to the barn for threshing and winnowing.

Harvesting is what our labour in the sixth house is about as well as taking stock. We are required at this stage of our journey round the wheel to examine how we work, adjusting our procedures if necessary. We must also check our tools and instruments, and those that are faulty must be repaired to improve their efficiency. For the same reason we must heal what is infirm in our body. Then, having put things right, we can continue on our way.

As harvesters we reap we what we have sown, and the sixth house is also known as a karma house, so what we experience here will be to some extent the result of our past decisions and actions. For example, if we have over-taxed our body with a lifestyle that was too stressful, we are going to suffer the consequences now. Or, if we have been over-extravagent and spent our savings, now is when we will have to tighten our belt. We will also be required to right any wrongs laid to our account, as Hercules had to right the wrong he did to Hippolyte before returning home.

The contrast between the mood of the fifth house and that of the sixth takes some getting used to. It is as if the high volume of our self-expression is suddenly turned down so we can hardly hear ourself, and a role reversal occurs when we leave our position in the spotlight to join the chorus line. Instead of being the star, we are now required to play a supporting role in the drama of life.

Whereas in the fifth house we needed to make our mark on the world, we lose this ambition now, and rather than having too much ego we seem to have too little. But appearances can deceive. The ego is likely to be still there, but hidden. It shows its face when we are proud of how humble we are, and when we see ourself as more spiritually advanced than others, as we are purer than them in thought and deed.

Separating the Subtle from the Gross

We have reached the second point of the earth trine (Fig. 11, page 32) and the second point of the mutable cross (Fig. 14, page 45). As fixed energy gives way to mutable, rigid attitudes dissolve and become more pliant, and once again Mercury acts as the catalyst. In the third house he stimulated our intellectual curiosity, and led us beyond our fixation with material things. Now, as sixth house ruler, he leads us beyond our obsession with expanding our power and importance, allowing us to experience a looser, more flexible way of being.

Mercury stimulates the mind, so we start analysing and inquiring into things again. Our attitude to life is a sceptical one, and we will have to be convinced by hard facts before we believe in something. We will also turn our analytical mind upon our self, and it is through our self-questioning that we lose the naive self-belief we had in the fifth. Instead of being self-confident we become self-conscious, and instead of expanding in trust we shrink in doubt - unless we learn to use the mind to maintain a level of continuous awareness. Then we will be able to stay both in our energy flow and in the mind at the same time.

In mutable earth Mercury's rationality is experience-based. For example, we like our science applied rather than theoretical. But expressing in earth - the densest and heaviest of the elements - Mercury who is so light and airy by nature can feel uncomfortably trapped, unless he transmutes earth through raising its vibration.

The alchemists used Mercury in the form of quicksilver for this purpose, believing in his power to dissolve the fixity of matter. Ostensibly directed to transforming base metal into gold, their work had an inner level that was concerned with refining the gross in the human soul. Through a process of purification and refinement they aimed to raise the vibrations of both matter and mind to a higher spiritual level.

The evolutionary path through the astrological houses parallels the progressive stages of the alchemists' great work - the sixth house corresponding to the stage of differentiation. At this point the elements are separated one from another. "Thou shalt separate the Earth from the Fire, the subtle from the gross, softly, with great ingenuity," was the instruction of the great magus, Hermes Trismegistus. Thus our sixth-house labour involves discrimination. We dissect and, through a careful process of analysis, separate the parts out to attain greater clarity of vision.

The Inner Virgin

If our natal sun is in the sixth, whatever sign it is in we will have a side that is like a Virgo, and express the Virgo archetype through a desire for perfection. Unless there are contra indications, we will be neat and clean in our habits. Our house will be tidy, and the flowerbeds will be weeded in the garden and the lawn mown. We cannot relax when there is mess and disorder around us.

Our need to keep our physical environment under control has to do with feeling safe in it. Creating and maintaining order can then be a full-time job. We will have folders and files to store our data in, and clearly labelled pigeonholes for our odds and ends. We will sort and store our clothes, books, kitchen utensils and any item that could come in useful. Our storage system will have its logic, so we will be able to put our hand immediately on any item we need. This is our strategy for warding off chaos, the arch-enemy ever threatening to envelop us.

With maximum efficiency as our objective, the technology in our home will be energy-efficient, and we will be economical with our resources and our time. We will make sure we know how to perform a job properly - as there is always a right and a wrong way to do things. And we will have the right gadgets or tools handy for the task, and return them to their right places afterwards.

But while our hands are busy working, our minds are also busy. They are mulling over our problems, which often concern planning for the future as we like to be prepared for any eventuality. And then there is the perennial worry about our material security to occupy our mind, as well as fears to do with our health. Our ideal of perfection also includes having a perfectly healthy body.

With Mercury as our ruler, we are mentally alert and verbally articulate, and we like to learn new things. We also like to teach - to pass helpful information on to others, and to correct them if they get their facts wrong. Our manner generally will be kind and amenable, and we will perform small acts of service to others gladly and care-fully. Nature plays an important role in our life, and we take pleasure in observing and tending plant and wildlife, taking delight in the beauty of many little details that others fail to notice.

Perhaps it is because we tend to focus so much on particulars that we can lose sight of the bigger picture. Then we are overwhelmed by a multitude of seemingly unrelated details, facts or instructions, and panic because we seem to be losing control. So our work of discrimination in the sixth includes learning to distinguish between what is important and what is unimportant. This allows us to set priorities, and decide which jobs to do first. In the same way we approach our ideal of perfection through distinguishing between the wholesome and the unwholesome.

So we make a distinction between the corn that we eat and the husks that we bin, and learn to recognise what is good for us.

And what has all this to do with Hippolyte, queen of the Amazons? She was the virgin queen, and thus perfect in the sense of unsullied by sexual contact with a man. Also, she and her Amazon women were complete in themselves in the sense of not needing a man to complement them. But the ideal of virginity is difficult to maintain - hence her girdle that was a kind of chastity belt.

The Devil and Idle Hands

In the sixth house we relate to our environment through our work, which gives us our social role and identity. We have a lot to contribute - our skills, for example, our expertise and our practical, hands-on approach to getting a job done. As we are perfectionists, we can be relied on to perform a task to the best of our ability. But the reason we put so much energy into our work can be because we seek validation. Here in the second trigant (Fig. 7, page 13), it is important how others see what we do, and their reaction to what we achieve can be crucial to our self-esteem in the sixth.

The traditional grouping together of work and health as sixth-house matters is explained when we understand that we need to work to stay healthy. The mutable energy here makes us tense and wound up unless we move with it, and working is a way of keeping moving and doing something useful at the same time. Usefulness is our criterion by which we judge whether something is worth doing or not.

So we can be fulfilled by performing a low-profile task, that fifth-house people for example would shun, if we can see it as useful and necessary.

However, when Saturn is in the sixth, we are likely to be resentful and feel put upon if we are always left with the chores. When we have to do menial work at our work place, while the more interesting, creative projects are given to others, we can become grudging. Then we see ourself as a Cinderella, made to slave away at the kitchen sink instead of going to the ball, and our deep-seated negativity towards ourself and our abilities is strengthened.

Even though we may have put up with this state of affairs for a long time, during a Saturn transit it will begin to feel unbearable. Saturn makes the shoe rub so it creates a blister, which makes us realise that we need to throw these old shoes away and buy new ones. In other words, it is time to change our pattern.

Our first step in this direction is to stop focusing on what others are doing and saying, and look at ourself instead, because the cause of our dissatisfaction lies not outside us but within. It is not because our efforts are going unappreciated, or because we are being treated unjustly that we are dissatisfied, but because of our underlying dependency on others for validation. Because deep inside we do not value ourself or what we create, we need recognition. So, for us to feel worthy, our work must be appreciated and our usefulness acknowledged. If this does not happen, it proves our own lack of love towards ourself, as the way others treat us always mirrors our own inner attitudes.

When we have Saturn in the sixth in our birth chart, we will have a pattern of playing safe. For example, we will stay in a job that is secure, but monotonous and limited in scope, rather than risk aspiring to work of a more challenging and interesting nature. If we are stuck in this way, and want to change the attitude that is preventing us from moving on, we could try internalising some helpful affirmations.

For example, we could programme ourself with ideas like "Just being myself I am worthy", or "The value of my work is in itself and not in others' eyes". But we must also be aware of the negative beliefs we carry inside, as they may have the power to cancel out these positive ones.

We should also be aware of being sceptical about, or openly critical of, other people's achievements. If we withhold recognition of the work produced by others, we indirectly withhold self-recognition, because on a spiritual level there is no separation between self and other. We are all one. So, if we can appreciate without judgement what others are offering as their contribution, what we contribute is more likely to be appreciated.

Health, Wholeness and Holiness

When it is in a state of worry the mind is a health hazard, and Saturn in the sixth can indicate a habit of worrying. Worrying means dwelling on negative expectations about the future. For example, the Amazon women had a negative expectation about what Hercules and his men would do when they arrived on their island. Because of it they armed themselves, which led to the battle and to their queen being killed. Because in a sense we create our own reality, our expectations can become self-fulfilling prophesies. Therefore central to our labour in the sixth is the work of transforming worry into trust.

As the sixth house is the house of health, health is often the subject of our concern. But our ruler Mercury is a healer and the patron of apothecaries, who use his staff - the caduceus - as their emblem. He works to strengthen our understanding of the relationship between our mental and our physical bodies, helping us to be aware of the psychosomatic link between them. Because of this link, our negative thoughts can have a detrimental effect on our body's condition. Thus, when we suffer a health breakdown, - for example during Saturn's transit of the sixth - it becomes crucial to change the habits of mind that lie behind it.

For example, we could develop a painful form of arthritis of the hip. Saturn is transiting our sixth house, bringing in the energy of the conservative Capricorn archetype, and we go down the route of conventional medicine. We have a hip operation followed by a course of drugs, and find that, although the problem in our hip is eased, other joints in our body consequently become inflamed, and the drugs have unpleasant side effects.

We thus discover that these methods alone cannot restore our health. When part of our body has fallen into disorder, coherence can only be regained through restoring physical, mental and emotional balance. A body can do this for itself in time, if it has enough strength and the right support. So interventions that stress it more than support it should be kept to a minimum.

In contrast, many gentler alternative therapies can give the body the support it needs. What helps most, however, is to increase our body-awareness, so we learn to listen and react to it. All in all we are required to take responsibility for our sickness and our health, which is presently not encouraged by the mainstream medical profession. And this habit of mind needs to be changed.

Experiencing a health problem is a hard challenge, but it can be just what we need in the sixth house, if it teaches us to look beyond the parts and see our organism as a whole. This is the second stage of our alchemical work. After we have separated out the parts, we must put them together again to achieve a holistic perspective. Becoming aware of how body and soul form one entity, we understand better how disharmony between our thoughts, feelings and physical needs will negatively affect our health. This can then lead to us making adjustments in our life-style.

With Saturn in the sixth we could be working professionally in the fields of conventional or complementary medicine, in which case we will be dealing with other people's health problems rather than our own. However, health, ill-health and adjustment through healing practices will still be our central issues, and our primary task will always be to heal ourself.

What we are striving for in the sixth house is balance - not only within ourself but also in our relationship with our surroundings. We need to be moderate here and keep to the middle of the road. Temperance, an old-fashioned word referring to an old-fashioned virtue, is a key in the sixth, because any extreme behaviour will stress our delicate nervous system and so should be avoided. Opening the heart centre is also vital as, unless we are open to giving and receiving love, our caring for others will have no warmth to it, and our service will become cold duty and mechanical routine.

Hippolyte's Girdle

An ideal of purity can be expressed negatively as exaggerated perfectionism, which leads us to always focus on what is wrong so we become blind to what is right. Then we go through life in fear of not measuring up to our own superhuman standards, and blaming ourself when we fall short of them.

Obsessive perfectionism arises when we try to apply an ideal of spiritual purity to our life in this far-from-perfect world. Originally it may have derived from religious beliefs that we no longer hold, but which are still affecting us unconsciously. Then we see imperfections in ourself and in others as sins, and it becomes our moral duty to draw other people's attention to their shortcomings, which always creates stress in our relationships.

Our striving to be perfect has taken us out of our heart and into our judgemental mind. Then our perfectionism can easily become an ego-trip, because we reinforce our ego every time we condemn another person, indirectly presenting ourself as holier - in the sense of more perfect - than thou.

The whole may be perfect, but the part can never be so, because the very fact that it is a part implies incompleteness. And when we have accepted this truth, we can relax. Those things that we saw as imperfect no longer worry us, and we no longer believe it our duty to improve them, because we trust that they have their rhyme and reason within the patterning of the greater whole.

Hippolyte's girdle as a symbol of virginity is also a symbol of wholeness. And in the sixth house, like Hercules, we feel it our mission to try to seize it. But, as we strive for it, we sully and blemish what we value. Hercules snatching the girdle is a metaphor for rape and, it is tragic that, in his eagerness to attain the object of his desire, he should slay his complementary female principle.

The law of karma then requires him to balance this deed, and a second virgin crosses his path. The sea serpent that arises out of the deep and swallows them both stands, like his fight against the Amazon queen, for sexual passion. This time they both emerge alive. Thus, by saving the maiden from the belly of the monster, Hercules renews her virginity. It is an act of ritual purification, that is also an act of love, through which Hercules pays his karmic debt and can then move on.

The Seventh House

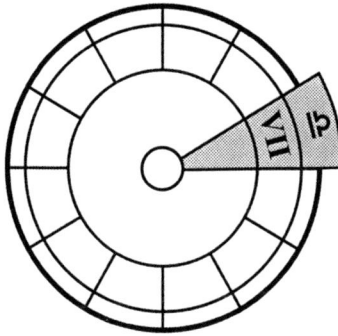

Capturing the Erymanthian Boar

Hercules' next task was to capture the Erymanthian boar. On his way to hunt it, he met his friend Pholus the centaur who invited him to share a meal. While they were eating, Hercules asked for some wine, but Pholus explained it belonged to all the centaurs in common. Undeterred, Hercules opened the wine jar. When the other centaurs arrived, they were furious to find him carousing on their wine, and threatened him with uprooted tree trunks. But Hercules laughed and, shooting his arrows at them, chased them away. Afterwards he found that one of his arrows had killed Pholus. Thus Hercules, sorrowing, had to bury his friend before proceeding to hunt the boar. He chased it round and round Mount Erymanthus until, exhausted, it hid in a thicket. Then Hercules took out the net he had brought and, prodding the bush with his spear, drove the boar out into the net. He then bound it and carried it on his shoulders back to King Eurystheus.

Out of Discord comes the Fairest Harmony

On reaching the cusp of the seventh house we emerge from below the horizon into the upper half of the wheel and enter the third quadrant (Fig. 6, page 12). On our journey through the lower hemisphere we have been discovering ourself and laying our personal foundations. Now, at this turning point half way round the wheel, our attention shifts from the self to the other, and our partners, opposite numbers and other halves become more interesting than we ourself are.

It is in this part of the wheel, lying furthest away from the ascendant - the seat of the self - that we see symbolised the sides of our personality that we least identify with. But the sign on our descendant[1] - the seat of the other - is often prominent in the charts of our partners and opposite numbers. The energy we meet here appears alien and interesting, and is attractive to us for this reason.

We associate with sunset the burst of fiery colour the sun radiates as it sinks on the western horizon. The ancient Egyptians worshipped the setting sun as the god Tum, honouring it as it disappeared below the horizon to continue its nightly journey through the underworld. In the yearly cycle, sunset corresponds to the autumn equinox when day and night are held in balance, and both are times of celebration and relaxation. With all her multiplying and

---

1 The descendant sign is the sign lying on the western horizon in a chart, and the descendant degree is the same degree as the ascendant in its opposite sign.

fruit-bearing done, Nature celebrates in a grand burst of autumn colours before relaxing into her winter sleep and, after we have ceased our daily toil, we relax at sunset into our evening leisure time.

The burst of fiery colour is felt in the seventh house as the pressure to take action and get creative. We are in an angular house again, and the quality of the energy is cardinal. But we are also under the rulership of Venus, and there are echoes here of the second house where Venus also ruled. There her prevalant mood of receptivity and relaxation was in tune with her ideals of love, peace and harmony. And these are also present as needs in the seventh house, though contradicted by the dynamic cardinal energy to produce a tension of opposites. As a result we tend to show a smooth, easy-going surface, while underneath we are far from relaxed.

"Opposition brings concord. Out of discord comes the fairest harmony," wrote the sage Heraclitus, an axiom that sums up our seventh-house labour. Interpreted, it means that antithetical principles generate energy through the tension arising between them, and this energy can be used to transcend their duality.

So, for example, in the seventh house where the energy is yang and cardinal but our ruler, the goddess Venus, is a real woman if there ever was one, we experience the clash of yang and yin. Also Mars' first house lies opposite Venus' seventh, intensifying the dynamic polarity between the sexual contraries. But from the tension between them we can create the fairest harmony. To do so, however, we need first to define and polarise our male and female sides. Each must be expressed fully and distinctly before they can be brought into balance with each other, and this is on our seventh-house agenda.

We can use the communicating and connecting skills we developed in the third house for this purpose, as we are now at the second point of the air trine (Fig. 13, page 44) and therefore linked to the first point energetically. Our communication skills, however, are now moving on a stage. In the third house we liked to hold monologues. In the seventh we enjoy listening as much as speaking, and this helps us to initiate relationships.

The Art of Dialogue

When your sun is in the seventh house, and there are no contra indications, you'll be a sociable extrovert. Like a typical Libra, you'll be able to talk easily and fluently, and have a genuine interest in people. For example, you'll be able to strike up a conversation with strangers on a train, who feel so at ease with you that they tell you the story of their life.

It isn't hard for you to make friends, and your pleasing looks and manner will also help you to be popular. But you are going to need a significant relationship - a best friend or partner to share things with. You define yourself as a part of a couple, and when you go anywhere it is important to have someone at your side.

Venus, your house ruler, will make you attractive as a sexual partner, so that when one relationship is over you won't wait long before you find another. And it is right and proper that this is so, because learning relationship skills is at the top of your seventh-house agenda, and you cannot practise relating without a partner.

You are also an aesthete and a person of taste - someone who pays attention to the details of his or her appearance. For example, your sense of harmony helps you choose colours and fabrics that match, so your clothes look right, and the way you wear them always looks good. It is all part of your deep need to create beauty, and you have many ways of beautifying your surroundings. Your love of beauty could also inspire you to become an artist or a musician.

Justice is another of your ideals. You have a developed sense of fair play, and are often asked to mediate in conflicts of interest between friends and family, because you are able to see both points of view. If it is your mission to bring more justice into the world, you could work as a counsellor or a magistrate. In such roles your ability to calmly apply the cool light of reason to emotionally fraught affairs can do a lot of good.

Because the seventh is an airy house, you tend to live in your mind and find decision-making hard. The mind by its very nature is divided, which is why you tend to prevaricate, spending too much time weighing up the pros and cons before you come to a decision. Deciding trivial mundane things is as hard for you as making life-changing choices. So, when you go shopping, you're likely to take your best friend or partner with you to help you decide what to buy. The trouble is that you can be so swayed by their opinion that you purchase what they want rather than what you would really prefer - so great is your need to please them by paying them the compliment of following their advice.

Anger is a No-no

When our sun is in the seventh house we need to be surrounded by love, and for this reason go out of our way to avoid a quarrel. If someone gets angry with us, even though we believe we are in the right, we will try to defuse the situation and calm them down. We find the rough and violent energy of anger stressful - too much for our sensitive nerves to bear - and it also offends our taste as it is unaesthetic. We keep our own anger well out of sight and out of mind. But, when others become aggressive, it is in danger of being sparked off, which we are anxious to avoid. So we will suggest making a cup of tea, and get them to sit down and discuss the problem in a rational, civilised way, thus returning to our home ground.

In many cases this works, and problems in relationships can be sorted out without the mutual wounding that expressed anger always leads to. But our overriding need for harmony can make us two-faced, so we smile when inside we feel hostile, and say nice things to people who we heartily dislike. Also, Mars energy however rough and rude cannot be excluded indefinitely. Though repressed it is still part of our nature, and is therefore likely to erupt in our relationships through being expressed by partners. The law of projection means that we must confront in others what we disown in ourself.

So in the seventh house we should remember that the other is holding up a mirror to show us the sides of our personality that we still need to integrate. In the seventh house, in order to re-claim our disowned qualities, we must enter into a dialogue with the other, a process that will empower us by making us more whole.

Perfect Equlibrium

If I dominate in my relationship, then the scales will tip to my side and, if I allow my partner to rule me, they will tip in his direction. I will be too light then to balance him out. The ideal partnership therefore, one of true equality and reciprocity, is symbolised by the Libran scales resting in perfect equilibrium.

The condition of being out of balance is often found at the start of a seventh-house partnership. Then the other becomes the axis around which the seventh-house person revolves. She keeps the relationship going through self-sacrifice, but becoming a player in the life of her partner, rather than having a life of her own, brings her into a position of dependency. Then, if her partner decides to leave her, she will feel she has nothing and she is nothing.

A Saturn transit in the seventh is likely to bring issues like these to a head. Saturn's name derives from the sanskrit word 'sat' meaning truth, and his mission is to destroy our illusions and show us things as they really are. So, during a Saturn transit of our seventh house, we could recognise some home truths about our marriage or relationship - truths that until then we have been unwilling to see.

Perhaps we believed in the romantic version of our story, and saw ourselves as a couple deeply in love. But now we are waking up to the painful fact that love has fled. Our partner's treatment of us is anything but loving, and our hidden anger has grown to the extent that it is blotting out the love we have in our heart. Up to this point, we may have given our family and friends the impression of being a happily married couple, but now the truth comes out, and others come to know that our marriage is on the rocks. Thus Saturn puts us under pressure to see the reality of our relationship and accept the consequences.

We may also have boundary issues outside our primary relationship, in which case Saturn will draw our attention to them. Many seventh-house people have a problem with saying 'no', when they are not yet grounded in their own being. They are unable to set others limits and defend their space, and are weak at making demands and getting their needs met. To become rooted in a solid sense of self was our first-house labour, which, if we have failed to fulfil, means we will be at a disadvantage when we arrive in the seventh. So first things first! We must repeat our first-house lesson to become capable of holding up our end of a relationship, and bring our scales into balance.

At this stage on our evolutionary path we are progressing from an 'I-consciousenss' to a 'we-consciousness', which means that, instead of me getting my way or the other getting his way, we get our way. Our seventh-house task, put in a nutshell, is to find the middle road between the extremes of selfishness and self-sacrifice, and for this we need our sense of justice. When the scales balance, this means our will and the will of our partner have equal weight, and giving is balanced with taking. This delicate state is achieved through practising compromise and cooperation. We moderate our own wishes and needs to accomodate those of the other, so that justice may reign.

All You Need is Love

Venus believes in making love not war, whereas Mars is so much into making war that he makes war when he makes love. Below the horizon we went through a step-by-step process, initiated in Mars' first house, of developing an ego and becoming a separate self. Now at the descendant this is reversed, and we start the complementary process by which, step by step, we surrender our ego and with it our sense of separateness. The first stage is to surrender in love to another human being which, if we do totally - though only in moments - can give us a glimpse of the transcendent consciousness described by mystics.

In the seventh house, love is the highest value and, if we think we have found it, we are ready to sacrifice a lot to keep it. We would give up our family, our career, our friends or our home for the sake of a partner. Sometimes we become a love addict, which means we fall in love with love. Then we need the constant high of being in love like an addict needs his fix, and suffer withdrawal symptoms when love departs.

But love in human life is ephemeral and comes and goes. Sometimes we discover that what we thought was love was in fact something else - perhaps need, pity, or the fear of loss. Thus we go through a multitude of experiences in the seventh that teach us what love is not, which prepare us for discovering what it is.

The seventh house is traditionally the house of marriage and, if Saturn is placed there natally, our failure to get to the altar could be a central issue. Although Venus rules love, Saturn rules marriage, because marriage is a security structure. Also, when we marry, we become a social unit under the law. So marriage can be defined as love legally sanctioned by society, and along with it come the expectations and the socially defined roles that restrict our freedom.

However, when Saturn is in the seventh natally, we often have a deep and irrational fear of marriage, which then prevents it from happening. We may have been scarred by a bad experience of marriage in a past life. Perhaps we were the unhappy spouse of a dominating and cruel partner, who imprisoned us in restricting circumstances. Then, however much we consciously want to be married, our unconscious fear of entering that state of misery again will prevail and prevent it happening.

Since the 1950's, the long transits through Libra of the disruptive outer planets - Neptune, Uranus and Pluto - have made marriage unpopular among those born under them, which is reflected in the high number of couples cohabiting without marrying as well as in the divorce rate. It has resulted in an increasing number of people going through life as singles. Perhaps this social group need a lifetime without a steady partner to recover from damaging experiences of marriage in their past, and to learn to enjoy their own company.

A Saturn transit through the seventh house can also bring a temporary period of aloneness. Someone who is emotionally dependent on being in a relationship may need a respite in order to return to himself. He can use it to learn to become independent at last, and may even discover that he can manage very well alone. Saturn has a habit of pushing us into the situation we most dread, thus giving us an opportunity to overcome the fears that were holding us back.

Many get married or co-habit in order to avoid loneliness, or need a partner to occupy them in order to escape from their own problems. But, if we have not first learned to be happy alone, we can never be truly happy with another. We need the independence of knowing that we can be happy both within a relationship and without. Then love will be freely given and freely received.

We may make creative use of a Saturn transit through our seventh house by deciding to work on our relationship, which automatically involves working on ourselves. Some couples go to couple counselling at this point, while others manage to thrash things out together. Saturn transiting the seventh is also a good time for coming to basic agreements and making contracts, as Saturn helps firm up the foundations of a relationship, making it a safe space in which mutual love and trust can flourish and deeper emotional roots can grow.

A relationship that is like a balanced pair of scales is only possible between two independent beings who have come together in love, and not because each have needs that they want the other to fulfil. D.H.Lawrence's image for the ideal relationship is a rainbow. In the novel of that name he describes an iconic couple standing like two pillars joined by a rainbow arch. In order to create a beautiful rainbow, man and woman must be polarised. Standing apart, each in their own space, they can be both deeply related and truly themselves. Then the rainbow of love flowing between them will symbolise yin and yang in perfect equilibrium.

In the story of the Erymanthium boar, Hercules has a partner - his friend Pholus. But the relationship is not a balanced one. Instead of listening to his friend and compromising, Hercules does what he likes. His action of helping himself to the wine is unjust as it breaks the law of the centaurs concerning common property. Instant karma follows and Pholus is accidentally slain. Hercules must then capture and bind the wild boar, standing for the selfish and brutish side of his nature that is responsible for Pholus' death. Once this labour is done and the boar has been bound, Hercules is redeemed.

The Eighth House

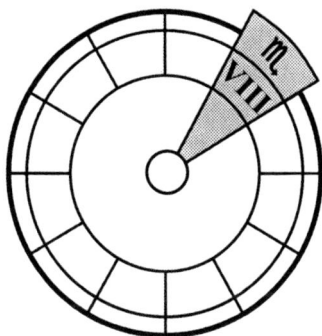

Destroying the Hydra of Lerna

Hercules is sent to the swamps of Lerna to kill the terrible hydra living there. First he shot flaming arrows into its lair to draw it out. When it emerged, rearing up three fathoms high and with all its nine heads hissing with rage, Hercules dealt it a great blow that severed one of the heads. But immediately a new head grew in its place, and so it went on. Then Hercules threw away his club and, seizing the hydra with his bare hands, raised it aloft. He held it suspended in mid-air until in the heat of the sun it dried out. When eight of its heads had drooped and died, Hercules cut off the ninth head that was immortal, and buried it still hissing under a rock. Then he returned in triumph to King Eurystheus.

Maintaining the Dam

In ancient cultures the eighth house was known as the house of death, because this western section of the sky was associated with the failing strength of the sinking sun. According to Egyptian solar mythology the sun died at sunset to enter the underworld below the horizon, where it traversed the regions of the dead to be reborn at sunrise. In this vein Greek astrologers saw the eighth house as the gateway to hell - hell in the pagan sense of Hades - but an eighth-house life can be hell in the Christian sense too!

In the yearly cycle, the eighth house corresponds to the Scorpio month of November, when in our northern latitudes darkness pervades over light. It is the season of death, decay and entropy in Nature. It is also the season of the feast days of the dead, and ghosts, ghouls and creepy things are called up on the night of Halloween. This is all relevant to our eighth-house labour which has to do with making friends with the darkness within us, and laying to rest the troubled spirits of our ghosts.

We have reached the second point of the water trine (Fig. 15, page 57), where the energy is also fixed (Fig. 12, page 33). Therefore, at this stage on our evolutionary path we must confront our most ingrained emotional patterns, and get to grips with our Id - Freud's term for the irrational, violent, eroticised and subversive forces of the unconscious.

Our fixity can be seen in the strength we bring to keeping these energies under control. It gives us the power to repress them, hiding them from our own and others' view - but only for so long. As the pressure builds up, as in water behind a dam, so our frustration increases. Finally, when bursting point is reached, the repressed passion becomes a storm surge flooding our rational mind.

So in the eighth house we experience repression and denial as well as catharsis and emotional release.

In classical astrology other people's money and values are the subject matter of the eighth. But we are in a water house here. So the emotional and psychological issues around others' money, possessions and values are what it's really about. In the second house we learned to stop clinging to material things. Now in the eighth we must let go of our moribund relationships, together with any unhealthy feelings from the past we may still be harbouring.

In the Underworld

We are going to encounter the underworld in some form in the eighth as Pluto is our ruler here. If it manifests in the outer world, we could be faced with issues around crime, fraud, extortion, drug trafficking, prostitution or the occult. But it could take an inner, subjective form, drawing us into those shadowlands of the unconscious where the hydra of our compulsive feelings, fantasies, obsessions and fixations has its lair. Of course, it could also appear on both levels at once.

As the eighth house belongs to the second trigant (Fig. 7, page 13) in which others are the focus rather than the self, we can encounter the underworld vicariously through other people. Then a criminal, an addict or a paranoiac person could enter our life, confronting us with the bad, mad or sad side of human nature in our close relationships. A sexual addiction may also be part of the equation, making us the slave of our passion, and giving us an extreme and intense experience of psychic forces that both fascinates and disgusts us.

Ultimately, the addictive relationships we move through in the eighth lead to us becoming wiser and more compassionate. On the way to emotional wholeness we must integrate not only what arises in our own soul, but also what we become aware of in others, because in reality we are all one. On a spiritual level there is no separation between 'I and Thou'.

Another alternative is when we are confronted with eighth-house issues in our daily work. This could be the case, for example, if we are a social worker or psychiatrist. We will gather manifold experience of how rabid psychic forces manifest destructively in other people's lives, and gain an in-depth knowledge of the dark side of human nature. Then, through bringing healing to our clients and patients, we can indirectly heal ourself.

A Good Friend and a Good Enemy

A natal sun in the eighth gives us strong qualities including commitment, purposefulness, and self-discipline. We are ready to fight our corner (the classical ruler is Mars![1]), and our dogged determination never to admit defeat makes us into a formidable foe. We are also strategists, using our water to intuit an opponent's motives and intentions. Our eyes have the power to penetrate surfaces and see what is underneath them. We are intolerant of

[1] Before the discovery of Pluto, Mars was the ruler of Scorpio and the eighth house, and can still be felt there.

deception and will create conflict on purpose to destroy the false facades that others construct, while at the same time keeping our own secrets well hidden.

The fixity of eighth-house water manifests in our habit of harbouring grudges and antagonisms - sometimes for years. So others are advised not to cross us. We will always avenge a wrong, and hit back harder than we were hit. Not only do we harbour negative feelings, we also act as catalysts and draw out negative feelings in other people. Thus we are good at making enemies. However, it turns out that all the time we are performing necessary evolutionary work - we are drawing what is dark, hidden and diseased out into the light, where it can be made conscious and be ultimately healed.

Our developed sixth sense that allows us to read the other like a book gives us the advantage of knowing where to strike in order to draw blood. But, like the scorpion in the animal world, we only attack when we feel threatened, or in retaliation for some past wrong. And, when we use our sting to wound, we do so believing that it is for the other's good - in other words that we are being cruel in order to be kind.

Our tendency to get entrenched in our emotional attitudes has a positive pay-off, as we can offer those we love an emotional security which is always valued. We are known as steadfastly loyal, and as always ready to protect and support our loved ones. The water of the eighth also gives us great powers of empathy, so we are capable of deep understanding and compassion. And when we fall in love it is going to be a serious affair. Our full emotional arsenal will be involved, and we will uphold our commitment till death do us part - and even beyond.

Loving Power and Empowering Love

When Saturn is in the eighth he mates with Pluto, and the archetypal mix can be deeply transformative, but first we will have a rough ride. Saturn brings a strong urge to control. So we are going to try to control our partner here, and issues of co-dependency will arise in our close relationships. We can use the psychic power that Pluto gives us to spell-bind and so bind the one we love to us psychologically, and in doing so we are likely to have a motive.

Because we are vulnerable to compulsive feelings such as jealousy, we must try to prevent him or her straying at all costs.

Jealousy is one of the larger of the heads on our inner hydra. For some it is the immortal head - the one we can never kill but only scotch. We live in fear of it as every time it bursts forth we become the torture victims of our own most painful feelings and imaginings.

For this reason, the strong willpower given to us by the Pluto-Saturn archetypal mix becomes the will to power. We need our power over others as we are deeply mistrustful and therefore on the defensive. Saturn in the eighth signifies that we have suffered betrayals of our trust in the past. We have been emotionally or even sexually exploited, and for this reason have closed down. The abuse could have occurred in past lives, but echoes of it may also have been present in our present life childhood.

If this is the case, we have a desperate need to keep our partners under control in order to prevent them from harming us. But we also want power over them to prevent them from running away, as we fear abandonment as much as abuse. However, if we believe our happiness depends on the other, and that we cannot live without him, then we will become co-dependent. Like the alcoholic and the carer of the alcoholic, master and slave are bound together by chains of need.

It is Saturn's job to bring these things to a head. So, crises can be expected in our love relationships during his transit through the eighth, and turbulent power struggles can be be played out to the point of emotional exhaustion or even death. The lesson we are learning is that power is a poor substitute for love, and that the only solution to a locked-in power struggle is love from the heart, rather than from the sex chakra or the power chakra.[2] It is time now for our heart chakra to open - and this opening is always painful. Finally, when our love has become generous instead of self-seeking, we will move from loving power to become powerfully loving.

Dying to the Old

Eighth-house people often have contact with the spirits of the departed. They are sensitive to places that are haunted, and may see ghosts. Some become mediums or therapists who work with spirit guides. However, when Saturn is in the eighth, great care must be taken to avoid

2 The chakras are energy centres in the etheric body.

damaging experiences in these areas. Saturn placed here can indicate residues of negativity in us that can attract malignant entities. So, before entering these realms, we need to do spiritual work on ourself and purify our emotional body.

In the eighth house the death wish may be strong in us. It lies behind our various acts of self-sabotage and our self-destructive habits. Our usual attitude may be one of denial but, when Saturn is in the eighth, the tipping point is reached, and we are forced to confront what we are doing to ourself. This provokes a spiritual crisis in which a moral choice needs to be made. Either we choose the path of growth and spiritual evolution, which is arduous and uphill, or we continue down the slippery slope of degeneration and devolution.

In the eighth house the subject of death provokes both fear and fascination. In a wider sense, we die many times during a lifetime. Separations from loved-ones are like mini-deaths and, as we grow out of old structures and emotional patterns fall away, we die to our past. But, because of the fixity of the archetypal energy, the eighth-house person will only let go under duress.

At least one life-changing close encounter with physical death will be on our agenda when Saturn is in the eighth. So, if we are clinging to someone in the belief that we cannot live without them, we should take warning. This could be the very person that Pluto snatches away when he emerges from the underworld. Thus we must go through the experience we most dread in order to learn a necessary lesson - that, unless we relax our grip on those we love, death will force us to do so.

The experience of the death of someone close to us can also provoke a spiritual crisis in our life by throwing us into the black hole of existential fear. But this may be just where we need to go, if we are at that stage on our evolutionary path where we must find answers to ultimate questions. We could be learning to distinguish between wanton destructiveness and necessary destruction - as, for example, when the foliage dies in autumn to make way for the renewal of Spring - and understand that we must clear away our old, outworn attitudes to prepare for the new that is coming.

We fear death not only because it threatens the body, but because it threatens the ego-personality with which we are identified. The prospect of the extinction of the self can induce great horror and despair. But enlightened ones, who teach that death is an illusion, say we are not the self. We are consciousness, and consciousness never dies. Nor does love. So, if we are united through love with a dying person, and have the privilege of accompanying him or her through the death process, we share in a profound, transformative spiritual experience. A close encounter with death can carry us out of our minds into a deeper place in ourself - the place we seek through meditation that lies at the core of our being.

Dying upon a Kiss

Sex is the other big taboo subject long relegated to the underworld. And sex and death as themes are often merged in human experience, although they appear to be opposites. Poets yearn to 'die upon a kiss', and sexual orgasm is is called 'le petit mort', whereas death has been described by mystics as the ultimate orgasm, the peak experience, in which not only part but the whole of our energy is released into the cosmos.

Sex and death have in common that they both demand surrender from us, and both are gateways through which we can escape our ego-bound mind to enter a wider dimension of consciousness. It is through these gateways that incarnating souls enter the world at conception, and departing souls leave it at death. But Saturn in the eighth can indicate that we have a problem surrendering. Then we will be tense and fearful of letting go when we move into sex. This may be experienced vicariously, in which case we are drawn to sexually uptight partners, and their problems then become ours.

Puritanical attitudes brought over from past lives often lie behind sexual inhibition. And to a reborn Puritan celibacy will appear attractive as a familiar way out of the whole dilemma around sex. Thus he will use Saturn's power in the eighth to repress his sexual energy. But what is repressed doesn't go away. Instead it tends to emerge in sublimated forms that can sometimes be morally questionable.

Saturn passing through our eighth house in transit will bring issues such as these to a crisis point. Then the energy we have dammed up for years, and sometimes for lifetimes, can erupt in ways that disrupt our life. For example, our gentle, loving husband and father of our children comes out as gay. We discover he's been leading a double life, frequenting gay bars and clubs, while we believed he was doing overtime at work. Fearing that he has contracted HIV and could pass it on, we then face the terror of going with him for an Aids test. Or the reverred catholic priest, who his parish believed was celibate, is revealed to be a compulsive child molester. Being exposed forces him to face what he had been denying in himself, and induces a crisis of conscience that shakes the foundations on which he has built his life.

"Desire denied breeds pestilence," as William Blake wrote, and Freud confirmed that suppressed sex energy causes an unhealthy condition of body and mind. In the eighth house things must be brought to light, and what we have condemned, renounced and denied must be accepted. So our sex energy should be welcomed as the basic expression of the life force, which if we repress we will also prevent its higher manifestations. As the tantrics taught, closing the base chakra prevents the kundali energy from rising upwards and expressing in the heart chakra as love.

What we need in the eighth house is an open heart chakra so that we are capable of a sexual relationship that is also emotionally nourishing - strong but tender. And we can only love tenderly when we are in our hearts.

Bringing out the Inner Hydra

Defeating the hydra involves bringing the dark and threatening feelings we were repressing out into the open. If we do this we will find that, once in the fresh air and warmth of the sun, they will lose their power over us. This our key for dealing with the negative side of the Scorpio-Pluto archetype. We must remember that, as long as the hydra remains in the swamp, we are helpless to fight it but, if we can bring it out into the light, it loses its power over us.

Defeating the hydra is a vital stage on the way to becoming master of our emotions - our labour in the water houses. To this end, we move through a series of crises in the eighth house which lead us to confront what we have been repressing. However, as the energy is fixed, we can have a strong resistance here to making changes. Our marriage can be hell, but we find it impossible to leave our partner, and hang in there far too long. We may need therapy before we can take the jump, but we resist this too as we are secretive about what is inside us. Our life seems to be resting on the thin thread of our self-control and we fear that, if this should break, we would be lost.

In the eighth we can be in the claws of the forces of negation and fall into black holes in which our mood borders on total despair and we negate all positive values including love. But, having reached such a crisis point, this can be when we experience transformation. Suddenly we see a light at the end of our dark tunnel, and start moving towards it.

A strong regenerative power is found in the eighth house. It is the power that pulls the snake from its dead skin, and the butterfly from the chrysalis. And, after the storm has blown over, we are left floating in calm water, and can touch a deeper state of peace and acceptance than we have ever known before.

Thus we are brought to a crisis point where we either break down or break through. In this house of death we come to the realisation that it is the ego that must die, because it is the ego that has been powering our inner monster. Then, having done battle with the hydra, and passed unscathed through death and destruction, we bury the last head that is immortal, still hissing, under a stone, and rise again like Hercules triumphant.

The Ninth House

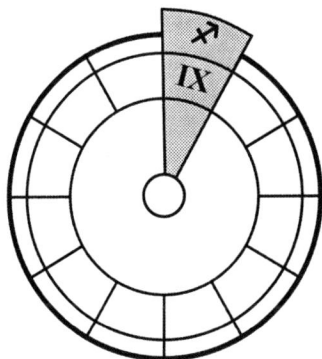

Overcoming the Stymphalian Birds

The Stymphalian birds were large, fierce and hideous, with feathers like steel shafts and beaks that could cleave a pate in twain. They terrorised the countryside around the marshland that was their habitat. So Hercules was sent to destroy them. His club was useless against them, and so were his arrows. Then he had a brain-wave. He fetched a pair of cymbals that gave forth a piercing, high-pitched sound. Having covered his ears with pads, he clashed them until the birds rose up in in confusion, and departed never to return.

On Top of the World

At the cusp of the ninth house, the arrow attached to the coiled snake in the Scorpio glyph breaks free to become the flying arrow of Sagittarius. Cleansed and transformed by the waters of the eighth, we now have a strong sense that we are on a path, and seek inspiration to carry us for-wards. This we find in the ninth house of mutable fire.

Fire is the most spiritual of the elements as it contains the essence of the universal life force. And the third point of the fire trine, standing above and between the points at its base and perfectly balancing them, creates a fiery isosceles triangle (Fig. 8, page 18). The flame of a burning candle takes on a triangular form. Whereas at its base the fire appears almost solid, as it rises it loses substance to become ethereal at the tip. Thus the flame is a symbol of transcendence.

We have been climbing steeply on our journey round the wheel, and have now reached a height from which we can survey the landscape spread out beneath us. This means our understanding ranges over a wider area of life, so we see things in their contexts. If before we were using a torch to explore life, we are now using an arc lamp, and, within the bigger picture, objects we thought of as sepa-rate are seen now to be connected.

The ninth house cusp marks the beginning of the third trigant where the house rulers are the giants of our solar system (Fig. 7, page 13). In this section of the wheel, the issues brought into manifestation by the archetypes tran-scend the narrow concerns of personal life to embrace transpersonal subject matter. We look outwards at our environment, and are conscious of our social context. We realise that we are co-responsible for the state of the world, and seek a social role through which we can par-ticipate and make our contribution.

But we cannot fully embrace a transpersonal cause as long as we are ruled by self-interest. Thus the full creative potential of the ninth can only be realised when the labours of the preceding houses have been performed, and the patterns behind our need for the ego have been transcended. In the third trigant the rule of 'first things first' must be remembered. Otherwise the unresolved problems of the previous houses will still be hanging over our heads, and will create a glass ceiling that impedes our arrow's flight.

However, on entering the ninth house, we are in no mood to notice ceilings. We are elated by our release from the fixed convolutions of the eighth, and the mutable quality of the energy here spurs us on, making us impatient to move into new experiences (Fig. 14, page 45). Mutable fire is like a hot air convector ready to carry us up and away. But where are we heading for, and why do we want to go there? These become the burning ninth-house questions.

In the Transit Lounge

Seen from the heights of the ninth where the world unrolls at our feet, opportunities appear to be opening up on every side. No wonder ninth-house people have itchy feet. Following the call of the beyond, they become jet-setters, back-packers or itinerant wanderers. Whatever their mode, and whether they realise it or not, they are on a quest in search of the meaning of life.

Their journeys can be physical or mental. Just as they are drawn to explore the far-flung corners of the earth, so their minds are attracted to explore new ideas and theories, and on both levels the same applies - wherever they are at soon starts to feel boring, and the grass elsewhere always looks greener. So a ninth-house life becomes a life in the transit lounge.

It is very unlikely that they will remain living where they were born and grew up, and many will live and work abroad. Other continents beckon from the travel brochures, and ninth-house people will travel the world on shorter or longer trips. They are at their happiest in foreign places where everything is new and open, and where, as foreigners, they are not expected to conform. Exploring some foreign city on their own, with no one to slow them down, they feel powerfully free.

Travel expands our physical and mental horizons. By removing us from our accustomed environment and depositing us in another, it distances us from the beliefs and attitudes with which we were identified. We gain a more objective view of our homeland, seeing the relativity of its values and social mores. Thus, through immersing ourself in different cultures, we gain different perspectives on life.

This experience of cultural relativity is a necessary one in the ninth, where our task is to get our beliefs and values straight. It is the preliminary part of our labour that must be performed before we can identify our goals. But the mutable energy of the ninth is a problem here. Although our fiery enthusiasm can carry us a long way, we are changeable and, initially at least, lack fixity of purpose. So like a weather vane we keep flipping and pointing in different directions, until, that is, we are able to consciously set our sights. Then we will determine our course and stick to it.

Looking on the Bright Side

When we have the sun in the ninth house in our birth chart, unless there are contra indications, we will have a lot in common with Sagittarians. Jupiter is our ruler and is always at our side ready to jolly us along. This means we will tend to think positively, and our basic attitude to life will be an optimistic one. We will need the feeling that we are making progress, and moving up a little higher with everything we learn or do.

We are likely to hold positive religious or spiritual beliefs. For example, we believe in a purposeful universe that is in the hands of a God with good intentions, or in a universal intelligence that knows what it is doing. Our tolerant and liberal nature rests in this basic faith in life, which also lies behind our talent for looking on the bright side.

Thus we are able to see both our mistakes and other people's in a positive light. "Life is a learning situation," we will say. "We learn from our mistakes," and "Nothing ventured, nothing gained!" This attitude allows us to give hope and support to others, and share our optimism with them together with our trust in the benevolent workings of the universe.

However, when we have the sun in the ninth, there is also a danger that we are being over-confident. Then, if we have failed to look deeply enough into a situation, our

123

cheery optimism could be misplaced and we lead ourself and others up the garden path. The reason for our errors of judgement is that we tend to live in the future rather than the present. Our mind is so wrapped up in our future hopes and dreams that we are not present to the reality of the here-and-now. But the grandiose castles we build in the air can lack firm foundations, and our greatest of expectations can come to nothing.

Growing into Wisdom

In the ninth house we are on a quest, and what we seek is wisdom. Here we are not requested to abandon the mind - just the opposite. The ninth house is traditionally the house of philosophy and higher understanding, the place on the wheel where, rather than being dropped, the mind must expand. We only become wise when we are open-minded and broad-minded. So what must be abandoned now is not our mind but its content of Stymphalian birds - that means our strident, aggressive and oppressive ideas.

In Mercury's third house we developed our ability to think rationally. There our reasoning was deductive and analytical, and we became good at taking things to pieces to examine their parts. We believed that, once we knew the parts, we would know the wholes they go to make up. But here in the ninth house we have the opposite approach - top-down rather than of bottom-up. In other words our method is one of synthesis rather than analysis, and we use our intuition instead of relying on reason alone. We believe that wholes are always more than the sum of their parts, and know that we have to think big if we want to understand the meaning of things.

Hopefully we have integrated our third-house skills before we embark on our ninth-house quest. Otherwise we are likely to be so focused on the general that we neglect the particular. Then we will make sweeping generalisations that have no basis in fact, and our theories will be wild and woolly and lacking in concrete facts to back them up. In such cases, having Saturn in the ninth could be a benefit as Saturn concentrates the mind. He alone has the power to nail us down and make us think straight. But his ministrations have a downside too, as our minds become susceptible to more limited and prejudiced views.

If we have natal Saturn in the ninth, it is likely that we grew up in a narrow-minded family environment, where we were conditioned with our parents' dogmatic beliefs, which closed our minds to alternative ways of thinking. Then we will enter adulthood burdened with attitudes that block our mental and spiritual growth - unless we are able to overcome the fears lying behind them.

When we have Saturn in the ninth, what we fear is moral and metaphysical uncertainty. Thus, even if we move beyond our family's inhibiting values, we often do so only to find another belief system and adopt it as gospel truth. Saturn in the ninth also indicates a tendency to get into missionary mode, and start preaching. The more people we can convince of the truth of our beliefs, the more secure we are going to feel about them. Thus ninth-house people are often found proselytising - at Speakers'

Corner in Hyde Park, for example, or on the internet in today's world.

If we belong to this group, we should inquire into what lies behind our need to convert others. We should also ask whether what we proclaim is derived from our own experience. We may have learned it from some teacher or from books, in which case it will not be of much value either to ourself or to others. Wisdom is never attained through second-hand knowledge gathered from other people's minds, but must always be the fruit of our own experience.

The ninth house, after all, is not an air house but a fire house. Therefore what counts here is our experience in the smithy of life, and not the products of our intellectual imagination. In the group of ninth-house people are found many priests and teachers who go on relaying borrowed knowledge all their lives, and what they convey often falls on deaf ears. But the words of those who speak from their own experience have substance, and can be deeply meaningful or even transformative to those who hear them.

Ninth-house people often choose the priest-teacher role, as they aspire to serve society through educating others and broadening their minds. However, they are not necessarily consistent in what they teach. Truth is in flux in this mutable energy field, and what was believed to be true yesterday will not necessarily be seen as true tomorrow. As we move into new experience in the ninth, and gain new insights, we come to see the relativity of all assertions. This allows us to transcend dogmatism and replace it with an attitude of ethical and religious tolerance. Then we can allow others the same freedom to choose the beliefs and principles on which they base their lives as we claim for ourself.

Seizing the Moment

When Saturn enters the ninth house in transit, he can have a stabilising effect and steady our purpose. But, if we are up in the clouds, he will bring us down to earth with a bump. Any far-fetched notions we were entertaining will be tempered now with a dose of sour realism. Of course we are going to resent it, as our future dream was keeping us going. But Saturn's bitter medicine is always good for us in the end because it wakes us up to the real.

Saturn in transit in the ninth will accentuate the fears lying beneath our cheery surface. We are likely to become cautious and hold back when opportunity knocks, even allowing it to pass us by. An experience of failure could lead us to inquire into our caution. Perhaps the path to our goal now appears too arduous, and we are not confident we have the strength to make it. Or we may be pessimistic about the future in general. Then, instead of moving into the new, we prefer to play safe because the risks involved threaten our security.

While Saturn is in transit in the ninth, we need to be aware of our deeper beliefs and expectations concerning the future, as these are likely to manifest. If we set out on a holiday with negative expectations, our trip could be disappointing, or turn into a seriously challenging growth situation instead of being fun. For example, if we are afraid of getting sick, or having our money stolen, or experiencing disruption at airports with long waiting times these unpleasant things are more likely to manifest. It's the law of the self-fulfilling prophesy.

Perhaps we will never set out in the first place, because we will see so many obstacles in our life that are preventing us from travelling. These will be mainly in our mind and be self-created. So in the ninth house we must be aware of how far we create our own future reality, because if we make a bed we will have to lie in it.

Setting our Priorities

The ninth house is traditionally the house of religion, which has to do with future aspirations in most faiths. For example, the kingdom of heaven Christians aspire to is believed to lie in the after-life. If we have Saturn in the ninth natally, we are likely to have either been born into a family with strict religious beliefs, or into one where religion was a dirty word. In either case - whether we grew up amongst religious fanatics or amongst atheists with narrow material values - independent thinking about spiritual matters was frowned upon. We were not encouraged to question our parents' assumptions and seek our own truth.

When Saturn is in the ninth, we take these matters seriously, driven as we are by a deep need to find certainty in religious and metaphysical questions. So we will reach the point where we start doubting and questioning the teachings of the authorities. We are not overtly rebellious, as in the eleventh house, but critical and we challenge assertions that do not tally with our own experience.

It is a big step to leave the safety of the fold and strike out on our own, as churches and religious groups offer a clannish security and support. However, when Saturn is in the ninth, the fold will begin to feel too narrow. Oppressed by consensus opinion and feeling suffocated, we will have to break out of it or lose our integrity. Thus we embark on the quest in search of our own truth.

As our view of life widens to take in larger contexts and frameworks, we gain an understanding of the power of collective opinion. We recognise how our lives have been formed by the dominant ideas of our environment. We see, for example, that we are influenced by the views fed to us by the media. This can lead to us making conscious choices about which newspapers we read and which TV programmes we watch. In other words we start taking responsibility for the contents of our mind, which is an important stage on our evolutionary path.

For the same reason the ideas that lie behind the social institutions of our environment also interest us. We may study law, education or theology, and thus gain an understanding of the principles and values on which the cultural establishment is based. Or we may focus on the arts and study literature, the visual arts or music, learning to value the educational and civilising potential of the great works of art of our cultural tradition.

We may discover our vacation in teaching and researching in these areas - a form of work that appears a worthwhile use of our time and talents, as we are expanding people's minds and furthering their growth. We can become a recognised authority in some intellectual or spiritual field, attaining a position of influence. In which case we must beware of abusing our power. Unless our ego has been sufficiently transcended, we may use our status to exploit others by setting up as a pseudo-guru. Then we manacle other people's minds by imposing our opinions on them, and use the adulation of our disciples to boost our self-esteem, and collect a load of bad karma.

The labour of the ninth is about determining our own values rather than the values of others. It involves seeking until we find our own belief system, and ordering our philosophical ideas so we can map out our life path. To this end we may take up astrology, which lends itself to this purpose. It alone of the arts and sciences is able to reveal intelligible patterns behind our individual experiences, and show how single events link up into purposeful wholes.

When we are secure in our understanding of life, we will be able to set our priorities in a way that makes the best use of our time and resources. We will be able to see our goals clearly and move towards them confidently. In the two previous mutable houses setting priorities was hard, as we were overwhelmed by details there, and so unable to distinguish between the essential and the non-essential. But now, given the grand overview of the ninth house, things fall into place if we allow them to do so.

Hitting the Centre of the Target

In the ninth house we have the energy and enthusiasm required to actualize our potential, but our creative force needs to be directed. It becomes crucial here to determine our goals and then move consistently towards them, so that our life has shape and coherence. If our mind is too scattered, it will prevent us from getting this together, as our actions will be scattered too.

A turning point is reached when we come to the understanding that we have a choice about how to use our time on this planet. Either we can develop our minds and expand our consciousness through following a path of spiritual growth, or we can squander our resources and waste our potential on trivial pursuits. In the latter case, we will remain unfulfilled and therefore unsatisfied. Our pleasures will be temporary and our underlying misery will be permanent. Fulfillment in the ninth lies in knowing that we are on our path and moving closer to our destination. And growing spiritually means continually surpassing ourself.

The Stymphalian birds represent strident and undisciplined ideas. A mind that is too full of them is like a marsh full of raucous birds that make a lot of noise. Hercules cannot defeat them by force, so he uses something subtler. The high-pitched note of the cymbals so concentrates the mind that all irrelevant thoughts fly away in confusion. Emptied of oppressive ideas, our consciousness is then like a sky empty of birds.

We centre ourself in the reality of the here-and-now and, attuned to the higher frequencies of meditation, like a Japanese zen archer we take aim... and shoot our arrow unflinchingly to hit the target bang in the centre.

The Tenth House

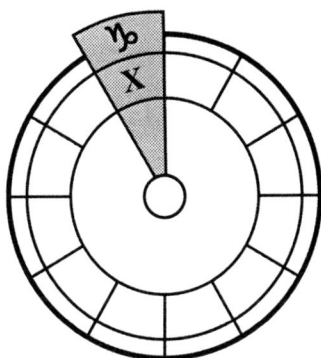

Overcoming Cerberus and
Freeing Prometheus

As a punishment for stealing the heavenly fire,
Prometheus was chained to a rock in Hades where a
vulture came each day to peck at his liver which then
grew back again. Hercules was sent to Hades to release
him. After crossing the river Styx, he found his path
blocked by Cerberus, the monstrous three-headed dog
who guarded the entrance to Hades. It leaped at him, but
Hercules was able to seize its primary throat and hold it
in a vice-like grip. The dog thrashed about until its
strength subsided and it grew limp. So Hercules passed
into Hades where he found Prometheus, and could break
his chains and set him free.

In Saturn's Chilly Realm

When we cross into the tenth house we enter the midday area of the wheel, where there is maximum light and shadows are shortest. Paradoxically, this corresponds in the annual cycle of the sun to Capricorn and the time of the winter solstice, when darkness is deepest in our northern latitudes. At this nadir point of the year the life force moves inwards. Trees are stripped bare, animals are in hibernation and many die of cold. Yet, although the winter solstice may feel like death, this is the moment when light is reborn.

Saturn, whose name means 'the truth', is our ruler in the tenth, and in his starkly lit house there there are no hiding places. Here we must face up to reality. On our journey round the wheel, Saturn has appeared to us as a hard taskmaster, so we may enter his realm with some trepidation. But we also know there are qualities of character we need to develop at this stage on our path that only he can teach.

In the ninth house we became aware of the collective mind as the ground of our socially conditioned beliefs and attitudes, and in the tenth we confront its manifestations in concrete form. We are out in the world now, and required to play a role in the institutions and organisations that structure society. Whether we like it or not, we are determined by these systems and our freedom is circumscribed by them. Either we accept being a cog in a wheel, or we rise to become one of the controllers. However, once in a position of power, we find we are locked within even larger wheels that are part of a great machinery of wheels within wheels.

In the tenth house we come under law in the sense of discipline imposed from without. Laws create the limits that are necessary in a society at our present stage of evolution. We are not loving and self-disciplined enough yet to live together without laws to regulate our interaction, and police to ensure they are kept.

When we incarnate on earth we succumb to the laws of nature that bind us as long as we are in a body, and the laws of the collective psyche that pattern our minds and imaginations. Thus human life by definition is subject to saturnian necessity, and our tenth-house labour involves learning to accept our limitations with patience. We must endure what cannot be changed.

Appropriately the feast of Christmas is celebrated close to the winter solstice. Born in a lowly stable among the beasts of the field, the Christ child symbolises the incarnation of divine light in densest matter. The Capricorn archetype that is active at this time of year is redolent with mysticism. And the earth trine (Fig. 11, page 32) where it represents the third tip, also dissolves into insubstantiality at its transcendent point. The apotheosis of the element earth is said to be experienced at the point of enlightenment when matter is spiritualised into light.

In the Public Eye
Once again, entering a cardinal house marks a turning point on our journey. It is at this final corner of the

cardinal cross (Fig. 9, page 19) that we start our descent along the eastern side of the wheel to pass through the fourth quadrant (Fig. 6, page 12) In this last phase of our journey, our focus moves beyond the self to embrace transpersonal dimensions, and we become increasingly aware of the greater wholes in which our life is embedded.

In the tenth house reality for us is the social and political environment in which we live and work. Our interest focuses on issues to do with our working life, and matters of economic and political import. We see ourself as part of the social machinery, with a responsibility to hold up our end and keep the balls rolling. Our reputation in the community and our status in society are also what concern us. We see the general public out there as our judges with the power to approve of us or to condemn us.

When an astrologer is interpreting our chart, he will look to the tenth house and medium coeli[1] for information about our career and the course it is likely to take. And, in the tenth house, we tend to find our identity in our professional capacity. This identification is strengthened, for example, in Germany where the custom is to formally cite a person's profession along with his name. This gives us a Herr Studienrat Meyer, for example.

Because we tend in the tenth to become married to our career, it becomes crucial to find work we love, and to love the work we find - otherwise we will remain miserably unfulfilled. We must see what we do as significant and of value to society, and we also need our achievements to be

---

1 The medium coeli is the high point that the sun reaches at midday.

acknowledged. The satisfaction of doing a humble job well, as in the sixth house, is no longer enough. What we attain professionally should be publicly recognised and rewarded with promotion, as our sights are always set on the next rung up on our career ladder.

But we can only give our best and achieve our most if we come to the tenth having learned the lessons of the opposite fourth house. Because, for example, unless we are capable of creating a nourishing home life, we will have nothing to counter-balance the stresses of our work. And, unless we have healed our inner emotional conflicts, we are in danger of becoming neurotic workaholics in the tenth.

Finally, the extent and value of our service to the collective will depend on whether we have developed beyond narrow self-interest. For example, a lawyer who puts earning a fortune before giving his clients fair service, or a company director who puts his fat salary before the welfare of his employees, need to revisit the second house before approaching their tenth-house labour. Because only when their greed has been transcended will they be able to embrace transpersonal values, and find their life's purpose in serving the community.

The social environment in which we find ourself is never a coincidence. Astrology demonstates how it reflects our inner patterns and our karma. For example, how we experience the world about us is shown in the tenth house of our chart. If Saturn is there, our environment could appear a cold, hard and impersonal place. We could feel like a wage-slave, under a yoke and forced to do our job because we have no other choice. We see ourself as tiny cogs in the great wheels of industry and commerce, useful only as long as we are productive, and after that to be callously binned.

Seeing ourself as a tiny part of the social collective can be depersonalising. Then we are defined through being a member of a certain consumer group, or of a certain income bracket. Our identity is reduced to the pin number we punch in when we go shopping. Thus our human individuality is lost and we become a cipher. Such depersonalisation needs to be balanced through nourishing personal relationships, which we should have learned to form in the previous houses on the wheel. Otherwise in the tenth we are going to feel lonely and emotionally alienated.

Maximum Security

With Saturn as our ruler in the tenth, we have a tendency to expect the worst, and our security in the face of threatening eventualities becomes a major concern. Thus we take what defense measures we can. This is where the insurance companies come in, those typical manifestations of the Capricorn archetype. In the tenth house risks are calculated. We strive to protect ourself against the blows of fate that could threaten our status quo, our concern being to protect what we have built up so laboriously. This biases our political leanings towards a conservative party, where the representatives of the Capricorn archetype congregate, dedicated to preserving what is true and tried because it is known and safe.

However, the more security we achieve the less free we will be. We find ourself barricaded into our own bastion. If we want to escape, we will have to look in rather than look out. Instead of keeping a suspicious eye on the outer world, we should inquire into our inner life in order to understand what lies behind our need for maximum security. Perhaps we will discover that what we fear is our inadequacy. Fear and mistrust of life are driving us, because deep inside we doubt in our power to rise to the challenge of living dangerously on the brink of chaos.

If we had confidence in our power to discipline ourself, much of the structure that we allow to be imposed on us in the tenth could be dispensed with. But, on the other hand, our spiritual growth requires us to pass through the experience of being bound like Prometheus to the rock. Suffering the limitations and strictures of the tenth house toughens us up and we learn to be patient. It seems that we subjugate ourself to the austerities of Saturn's yoke to prove that we are able to survive and overcome even in the harshest conditions.

Getting the Joke

If we represent the Capricorn archetype by being born with our sun in the tenth, we are likely to be armed with an array of strong qualities to see us through when the going gets tough. Unless there are contra indications, we will be able to fall back on reserves of patience, stoicism and stamina. An array of practical skills will be at our disposal, and we will be canny in a worldly-wise way.

This all helps to fulfil our material needs and achieve our worldly desires.

We are likely to value a high standard of living here because of the status it brings, and we have what it takes to achieve wealth and prosperity. However, we are also able to live in reduced circumstances, and then we take pride in managing on very little, and create an ideal of our asceticism. We are also good at pulling ourself up by our own bootstraps. So, those with the sun in the tenth can be a prototype of the self-made man, one who has risen socially and financially from humble beginnings through his hard work, self-discipline and dogged determination.

Because we are so responsible and reliable, others tend to look on us as their pillar of support. They value our practical, down-to-earth advice that is always based on a realistic appraisal of the situation. However, our attitude towards the weak is 'no molly-coddling!' It is our firm belief that everyone should stand on their own feet from a tender age, and become as autonomous as we ourself are. We can be merciless towards shirkers and lay-abouts, because an unproductive life in our eyes is a crime against society.

When tenth-house people go beyond the ego and sub-ordinate their personal desires to communal needs, they can lead the kind of exemplary life that was known in the past as the 'vita activa' - a life of service to the community. Having provided for their material needs and for those of their dependents, they then focus on the needs of the collective and, because they understand the laws of the material plane and can creatively apply them, may become great public benefactors.

In the role of the boss, however, they are stern and unbending. Severe in their judgements and autocratic when keeping order, their only interest seems to be to get the work done quickly and efficiently. They can also be wet-blankets and quash any displays of high-spirits and playfulness. So if we are a tenth-house person with an 'all work and no play' attitude to life, we will need to lighten up. Perhaps we are taking ourself and life in general too seriously - although sometimes streaks of our sardonic sense of humour will break through.

If negativity about life and human nature is our default attitude, we can lighten up by laughing more. Although tenth-house people are not good at the belly-laugh, concerned as they are with staying in control, if we practice the laughter meditation - which involves laughing deeply and uncontrollably for ten minutes a day - the world immediately becomes lighter and brighter. And, if we practise it in a group, this alleviates our tendency to isolation, as when we laugh together with others we become one with them.

The Path to the Peak

When Saturn is in the tenth, we choose to take the steepest and most direct way to the peak, and are ready to make great sacrifices to reach it. We may see the mountain top as representing the height of our worldly ambitions, but the mountain is a spiritual one and its peak stands for illumination. Whether we know it or not, this is where we are heading, and Saturn is helping us to get there by bringing to light the hidden fears that are impeding our progress. His method, however, is a brutal one as he always conjures up the very situations that we fear most.

For example, an economic slump and a rise in unemployment could exacerbate our fears around our material security. We may lose the nest-egg we had invested in the stock exchange, or the pension fund we were paying into could collapse. Another scenario is that, through no fault of our own, we are made redundant. We fail to find another job and have to go on the dole. In this case, being forced to scrape a living from a minimim income is not a big deal, as we are practised in forced economies, but our reduced status in society will be a big problem.

Or, if we remain in our job, Saturn in the tenth will test our endurance. We are likely to find ourself weighed down with more responsibility and extra work loads. Then, although our duties are onerous, we go on carrying the burden, driven by our fear of failing and being deemed incompetent. As we knuckle down and work long hours for very little reward, we realise that, to keep going and to keep our job, we must develop our powers of concentration and increase our general efficiency. And the result is that we develop the skills needed to get the work done in the most economical and productive way. We may even find ourself enjoying this challenge, and succeeding against the odds gives a great boost to our self-confidence.

Saturn in our chart always embodies what Freud called 'the superego' and, when he is found in the tenth house, it is likely that he manifested in one parent or the other. Then our mother or father appeared as a strict authority figure, one who demanded from us a high standard of achievement. If we have internalised this parent, we may be still trying to win their love by living up to their expectations.

Our superego is also likely to be reflected in our boss at work. He will appear to us as very sparing with his praise and very generous with his criticisms. We will go to great lengths to please him, projecting onto him the exacting parental figure whose love we are unconsciously trying to earn. This could make us into a high achiever, and spur us on to reach the top of our profession. But however successful we are we will never feel we've done enough to win mother or father's approval. The solution to this dilemma lies in our doing the inner work that is needed to release us from this mindset, which is one of the largest rocks blocking our path to the peak.

Nothing Succeeds like Failure

When we are under a compulsion to prove our worth, we live in a state of continual tension. What we fear most is failing, as this would then prove our incompetence. So we become a hamster on a wheel of continuous efforting. We may attain a top job together with the lifestyle that goes with it, but beyond the shelf with its array of hard-won trophies our life is hollow, and inside we remain unfulfilled. Thus, when we reach the top of our profession, it could be to discover that we are less happy and less free than we were before.

This is the point when Saturn arrives in transit to collapse our house of cards. A possible scenario could be that we make a mistake and are held responsible for the consequences, which leads to us being ignominiously dismissed from our post. We recognise the pattern in our life of a rise to power followed by a great fall from the rhyme of Humpty Dumpty. It is when Saturn is in the tenth that the time of the great fall is likely to come, and the higher we have climbed the further we will tumble down and hit the ground with a smash.

As eggs cannot be put back together again, this is the point where we are close to despair, and many then fall into deep depression. Thus Saturn transiting the tenth can bring a dark night of the soul when our world falls apart. But this is our winter solstice, and at the darkest time in our life we are also closest to seeing the light rise at the end of the tunnel. Sometimes experiences of failure, that bring with them humiliation and loss of face, are needed to cleanse us of the remnants of our ego. And, once we have accepted that this is so, our fall becomes a breakthrough instead of a break-down.

Waking to the Truth

Thus failure can further our spiritual growth. Experiencing how all we have built up can collapse overnight, and how our hard-won position can be lost, we come to question worldly achievement as a goal. At noon the shadows of illusion are shortest, and the time of maximum light is the time of optimal awareness. Thus, stripped of our outer accoutrements, we can now see ourself as we really are - including both our present incompleteness and our spiritual potential.

In the myth corresponding to the tenth house, Cerberus stands for the fears and illusions that block our path, preventing us from freeing our Promethean part that lies manacled. Prometheus bound to the rock in Hades is a metaphor for our fallen state of consciousness. When we incarnate in a body and are born on this planet, our consciousness is bound to matter. Then our awareness is restricted to the five physical senses and, without the light of spiritual fire, we live lives of suffering and limitation.

Prometheus was required to remain patient throughout his torture, and was finally liberated because he did not fall into despair. Thus when Saturn leads us through a dark night of the soul to the very edge of the abyss of life-negation, he does so to test us. In the face of failure and loss, we must not lose hope, but see our plight as conducive to our spiritual growth. Then our suffering can lead to enlightenment. When Hercules overcame Cerberus and set Prometheus free, he released the heavenly fire and light was reborn in the world.

The Eleventh House

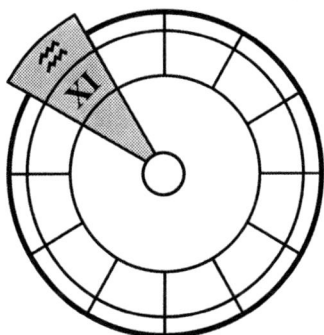

Cleansing the Augean Stables

The dung in the royal stables of King Augeas had not been cleared for years, and the filth was spreading a pestilence throughout the land. So Hercules was sent to clean them out, and was promised a handsome reward by the king if he could keep to the given time limit. On arriving at the stables, Hercules saw the enormity of his task. He set bravely to work but managed to accomplish very little until he had a brainwave. Two rivers happened to pass nearby, and Hercules was able to divert their courses so they flowed through the dung-filled stables and cleansed them. When the labour was done, the king refused him the promised reward, but Hercules replied that serving the people by saving them from pestilence was recompense enough.

A Bicycle Tyre Pumped up Hard

In the fixed air of the eleventh house our ideas and principles set like concrete. The conservative influence of
Saturn, previous ruler[1] of the house, can be felt here. The
establishment is established, and the status quo is stating
the quo, but Uranus - the modern ruler of Aquarius and
spokesman of the archetype - is also a strong presence.
His mutinous, zealous and erratic energy winds us up and
stirs up trouble. So, to navigate the eleventh house, we
must deal with the unpredictable cross-currents that flow
between these two giant forces.

No wonder eleventh-house people are paradoxical! On
the one hand they are freedom fighters and activists for
radical causes, who believe passionately in social justice
and condemn discrimination in any form. And on the other
hand they are disenchanted realists, with a bleakly rational
or coldly scientific approach to life's big questions.

The concept of fixed air (Fig. 12, page 33) - which we
can imagine as the air in a bicycle tyre pumped up hard -
explains why we become so set in our attitudes here. In a
fixed house we deepen, integrate and make sustainable
our experience from the previous cardinal house, so per-
sistence and continuity is required. But there is a limit to
the amount of air that can be pumped into an inner tube
before it either splits or the valve flies out.

In this culminating air house (Fig. 13, page 44), we are
set to continue the learning process of the air trine. For

1 Before Uranus was discovered in 1781, Saturn was the ruler of
Aquarius. Today Uranus is seen as ruler and Saturn as co-ruler.

example, we extend our communication skills to include public speaking, and widen our understanding of the mechanisms of social relating. But the superior point of the air trine, like the previous culminating points of the fire and earth triangles, is also a gateway to transcendence. If we practise meditation, we discover that we can step outside the mind and gain a distance to its contents - which is not the same thing as losing our mind! And this is the only way to loosen what William Blake called our "mind-forged manacles".

As we have seen, in the transpersonal trigant (Fig. 7, page 13) we are preoccupied with the concerns of society rather than personal issues. And in the eleventh house we are acutely aware of our social, political and, today, ecological responsibilities. We see ourself as part of our community, as citizens of our country, as members of the human family and creatures of planet earth. Slowly the illusion of being an isolated self loses its grip, as we recognise the widely encompassing systems that define us and in which we participate.

The Great Sky God

In the words of the song, we are at the dawning of the Age of Aquarius, and the activation of the Aquarius archetype can be increasingly felt in human affairs. Our paradigm of reality is going through a radical shift. In physics, for example, the discovery of the chaotic quantum flow, the ground of what we know as matter, has taken us beyond the mechanical world-view of Newton and Descartes. And systems science has appropriately developed chaos theory

- appropriately because Uranus, the spokesman of the Aquarius archetype, was grandson to Chaos in mythology.

On the quantum level, time and space no longer apply as parameters, and what we see as solid matter disintegrates into waves and particles. Physicists have proved that an act of observation has the power to collapse a wave into a particle in a way similar to a thought crystallising in the mind. In fact the quantum flow seems very like the 'anima mundi' or mind of God, containing in implicate state the ideas of all that has existed and will exist in the universe. In astrology we associate the universal mind with Uranus, the primeval sky god.

Thus the eleventh house opens onto higher mental levels, but to access them we must move beyond the deductive reasoning and logical thinking that Mercury represents. Astrologers see Uranus as Mercury's higher octave, as he stands for our capacity to think laterally and find solutions through using our intellectual imagination. Thus like Archimedes in his bathtub we can get a sudden brainwave, and in our excitement run out onto the street naked shouting "Eureka!"

However, if we think our brilliant ideas are our ideas and try to take credit for them, a serious ego problem can develop here, when we start believing we are a cut above others because of our genius. They are not our ideas. They are merely particles that have collapsed out of the universal wave function into our individual mind space. The most we can do is provide a channel for them, and thus be the means of bringing new insights and fresh perspectives into the world.

But, to use our flashes of inspiration constructively, we must stay grounded. This is not as easy as it sounds in the eleventh house, where contents from the collective mind continually flood our brain. These can unbalance us, making it hard to distinguish the wild and wacky from the sensible and practicable. As the saying goes, genius and madness are closely aligned and, once outside the rational enclave, we are vulnerable to being directed by unconscious collective impulses. But here Saturn's co-rulership of the eleventh house becomes a blessing, as he alone has the power to stem the flow and nail us down.

Changing the World

If we have the sun in the eleventh house in our chart, we will be like an Aquarius - split between Saturn and Uranus. On one side Saturn encourages us to seek safety in numbers, so we'll find some social set to identify with and we will keep its rules until, one day, Uranus appears from nowhere and pulls the rug from under our feet. Then, either our circumstances will alter unexpectedly, or we will get some bee in our bonnet that pressurises us to change our life.

For example, we could leave our home, our friends, our jobs or our partners suddenly and irreversibly. We may not understand why we are doing this. All we know is that the prospect of staying put has become unbearable. We are being swept along by a force beyond our control, and are ready to risk our securities to move into the unknown. A mood of desperation may be just what we need to carry us up to the next stage on our evolutionary path, but it could also be counter-productive, as we may recklessly destroy what we have built up, and throw out our babies with the bathwater.

With the sun in the eleventh, unless there are contra indications, we will have well-developed communication skills and be good at debate, as our approach to life is through the intellect. If we are expressing our Saturnian side, we could have a career as an academic scientist - one who sets high value on rigour and logical exactitude. In this day and age we will also be highly computer literate.

But, if we are expressing our Uranian face, we may become the kind of nerd who is into the wackiest latest technology, and who uses the computer to insulate himself from others and withdraw into a virtual, digital world. There he replaces flesh-and-blood friends with a virtual social life, finding like-minded people online and communicating with people who share his interests in chat rooms and online forums.

Another Uranian behaviour pattern is to drop out of straight society to take refuge in some extreme group or fringe movement, where we will find people open to listening to our passionately held views. But a proper discussion of them is unlikely to arise as we are unable to listen, and tend to reject outright all opinions contradicting our own. If this sounds familiar to us, it means we have not yet developed the art of conscious communication, which was our labour in the previous air houses. So - first things first!

If we have the sun in the eleventh, we could be so out of touch with our feelings that we are unaware of the emotions behind our pet ideas. We follow our principles rather than our heart and, when we support those who are being discriminated against or persecuted, our solidarity with them remains on the level of abstract ideas. We support underdogs not because we feel for them, but because we have a social conscience and a strong sense of justice.

In fact, in the eleventh house, we find it easier to love humanity than to love those human representatives with whom we are in close relationship. As Uranus makes us so absolute in our judgements, it can often happen that we quarrel with and separate from close family members and become estranged from partners. The eleventh house follows the eighth in the fixed cross (Fig. 12, page 33) and, if we have a pattern of breaking off relationships as soon as deeper emotional problems arise, it indicates that our eighth-house labour has not been completed. So we must return to sort out our water issues before rising into the airy stratosphere of the eleventh house.

Stuck in Mental Rut

When Saturn is in the eleventh house, we can become fanatically attached to our ideas. Then the views we adopt act like blinkers and narrow our field of vision. When our friends start to complain that we always harp on the same old themes, it's a signal that we are stuck in a mental rut.

If we ask why we have become obsessed with our social or political views, we are likely to discover that we have an emotional investment in them. For example, our personal disappointments in life may have coalesced into deep social grievances. Or our failures have left a chip on our shoulder, and instead of blaming ourself we are angry with the government. A woman could project her personal struggle against a dominating father onto society and become the kind of rampant feminist who takes up arms against the patriarchy. Or a man could start campaigning for paedophiles to be publicly exposed without realising he was himself sexually abused in childhood, as he has firmly repressed this memory.

Thus, if we have gone into mental spasm, the only way to free up our mind again is to inquire into the psychological roots of our emotionally loaded views. Fanatical beliefs around our religion, our race or the land of our birth could derive, for example, from ego-pride. It is a human weakness to expand the ego by identifying with the political party, nation, race or religion that we see as superior. However, this psychological mechanism is dangerous as it leads to wars and genocide. So it becomes vital to sort out our eighth-house emotional issues before entering the ideological eleventh-house level.

The Need to Belong
When Saturn is in the eleventh in our birth chart, we will mistrust people who have power over us, and react very sensitively when an authority figure tries to impose his will. If this trait shows up from an early age, its root could lie in past life experience. For example, if in a past life we were the victim of oppression and exploitation, we are likely to come into the present life with a grudge against people in power, and a deep fear of the same thing happening again.

Saturn has a way of bringing our fears to our attention through provoking situations that echo past traumatic events. Thus, during a Saturn transit we will have plenty of opportunity to witness how we react to authority figures, as they will appear in our life to bug us. But, before we get locked in a power struggle with them, we should remember the mechanism of psychological projection. The outer enemy we fight is always present somewhere in ourself. And, if we believe that a powerful figure is crushing us, this means that somewhere inside we are harbouring an inner tyrant.

Because we are ruled by both Saturn and Uranus, we have an arch-conservative within us bedded down with a revolutionary. The former becomes projected as the reactionary faction in society we rebel against. The latter projected can become the criminal element, and the terrorists who threaten law and order and the civilised values we uphold. These roles are interchangeable, as proved by the number of revolutionaries in history who later became reactionaries. And those who rise to positions of power within radical groups dedicated to freedom and democracy inevitably behave in ways towards their fellows that are authoritarian and repressive.

Our greatest fear when Saturn is in the eleventh is of being excluded from a group that we are dependent on. In order to avoid this happening, we may go to the length of sacrificing our integrity. Then we will make a show of professing our loyalty, and say the right things to demonstrate that we have the right attitudes, whether in our heart we believe what we say or not.

However, when Saturn arrives in the eleventh in transit, the following scenario could develop: a dominant member of our group starts doing things we strongly disagree with. We go along with this at first and say nothing, but the dominant person senses our inner resistance and starts to victimise us. We turn to our friends for support but they let us down. Instead of coming out on our side, they side with our foe. We realise then that we stand alone, and have the choice, either to recant and rejoin the ranks, or to leave the group and lose our extended family.

But there is a third choice. The pressure of being in this quandary could lead us to look inside and examine our patterns of group relating. Then we may come to the conclusion that we have been giving away our power. And, instead of blaming others and feeling like a victim, we could start inquiring into why we did this in the first place. This leads to the uncovering of the compulsiveness behind our need to belong. Following the trail back to our childhood, we may uncover there a primal wound to our trust. And exposing a wound is the first and most important stage in its healing process.

As a result of this growth in consciousness, we begin to take responsibility for the way others react to us, understanding that it always takes two to create a conflict. We may also notice now how group situations always mirror what is going on in our inner life, and realise that, on the level of spirit, there is no separation between the inner and outer world or self and others. We are all the characters that appear on the stage of our life. And, in the same way, we are all the characters in the myth - Hercules the hero and Eurystheus, the authority figure, and even King Augeas, the rascal with the dirty habits.

A Good Team Player

In the eleventh house we are sociable and gregarious. Our friends will have priority in our life, and we could value our peer relationships higher than our relationships with our family. We are also more vulnerable here to peer pressure than to parental conditioning.

Our greatest fulfilment is found in working together with a group of like-minded people for a common cause. And it is this basic need to find people on the same wavelength that leads us to accumulate the experience we need of group relating. Starting with our first socialisation at nursery school, as we go through life we gain varied experience of group interaction in circles of friends, amongst colleagues at work and as members of clubs and societies, each with their different group dynamics.

In order to perform our eleventh-house labour successfully, we must learn to become good team players, which means finding our individual role in relation to the group and harmonising with the whole. Whereas our seventh-house aim was to achieve balance and harmony in one-to-one relationships, in the eleventh house we strive for this same ideal in groups and associations. Good teamwork is demonstrated by the example of the jazz band. To successfully improvise, a band needs to be melded into one mind and one sensitivity. Then coherence happens as an expression of synchronicity, without any overt leadership or outer organisation.

If we have the sun in the eleventh, we will need to find a worthy cause with which to identify. In the nineteenth century socialism lent itself to this purpose, and in the twentieth century it was the dream of the communist utopia. Now at the start of the twenty-first century, seeing that neither socialism nor communism have succeeded in creating a better society, we are groping around for a new vision.

We still want to change the world, as we see only too clearly what is wrong with it. But, as history has proved, neither a revolution from within nor a war from without has the power to achieve this as long as minds remain the same. We therefore realise that, if we want to change society, we must change the individuals who compose it. And, after many failed attempts to do this, we awaken to the truth that in the final instance the only individual we can change is ourself.

The ideal we are heading towards in the twenty-first century is the holistic paradigm. In our new future vision, the family of man works together like a jazz band on a global scale in full awareness both of our interdependence and our oneness with all life forms on the planet. Although each of us is a unique individual, we understand that we are not separate entities but share in a collective mind that is like a quantum field of entangled particles.

We are also at that stage in our development where we experience the power of ideas to manifest in the world, and realise that we must take responsibility for the consequences of the views we hold. Cleaning out the Augean stables can be read as a metaphor for cleansing the mind of the beliefs that breed pestilence. In the myth, King Augeus was so fixed and resistant to change that he refused to clean out his royal stables. The stench and noxious bacteria this caused correspond then to the social poisons engendered by fanatical beliefs based on anger and hatred.

Hercules, acting like Aquarius the water-carrier - who serves others by carrying water from the river to the villages - was able to save the situation through having a Uranian brainwave. His act of diverting the course of the rivers, so they flowed through the stables and washed them clean, corresponds to those inspired actions of eleventh-house people that change the course of history. And, when Hercules had thus served the community, he departed unrewarded, as our eleventh-house labour requires us to serve without the expectation of any ego-reward.

The Twelfth House

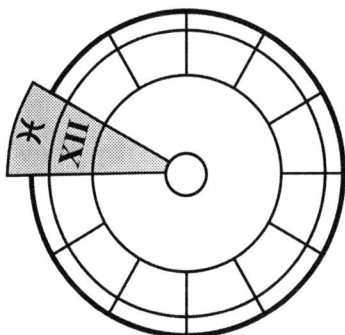

Capturing the Cattle of Geryon

Geryon, a terrible monster with three bodies, was unlaw-
fully holding a herd of red cattle and Hercules was sent to
capture them. They were guarded by a shepherd and a
fierce two-headed dog. As soon as Hercules approached,
the dog sprang at him. But Hercules slew him with a
single blow. At this the shepherd, fearing for his life, sur-
rendered the cattle, and Hercules departed, driving the
cattle before him. But soon he heard Geryon following in
hot pursuit. Then, taking aim, Hercules let fly an arrow
with such force that it pierced all three of Geryon's bodies
together, and killed him outright.

His journey home led across the Alps, where he had to
have his wits about him to prevent the cattle from straying. But he succeeded in keeping them together, and
delivered them safely to King Eurystheus. As a reward
for completing all twelve labours Hercules was made

immortal, and since then has dwelt among the gods as a constellation of stars.

Full Fathom Five

On the last stage of our journey round the wheel of life, we drown in the mutable water of the twelfth house. Our labour here is a spiritual one. We are required to surrender and let go of all we have been clinging to, but this loss of control brings up our fears. We have been living in the belief that we are someone - that we have a clearly defined identity - but this now seems an illusion. Like drops of falling rain, we are heading for the ocean below and, when we merge with those vast waters, the contours of our separate self will be lost.

Although on one side we yearn to lose our selfhood here, we can't help but cling to what we know as our ego. But the rule of the twelfth house decrees that the more we cling, the more we will suffer. And the suffering will continue until our hearts have opened to unconditional love, and we can gladly and patiently accept all the gifts that life brings - even the most bitter.

The final point of the mutable cross is also the transcendent point of the water trine (Fig. 14, page 45 and Fig. 15, page 57), and a point at which we either breakdown or breakthrough. Insecurity is present in all the mutable houses where structures we have been relying on are dissolved. But our insecurity is greatest in mutable water where the stability of the psyche itself is under threat.

Unless it is contained, water leaks out all over the place and drains away, and mutable water is the hardest to contain. So, as we move through the twelfth, it can feel as if we have lost our oars and are drifting at the mercy of the waves. The ocean surrounding us is an image for the universal psyche, and Neptune's submarine realm stands for the collective unconscious, flowing like underground water below life's surface, and connecting our individual psyches into one whole.

Neptune as the yin partner of Uranus, who stands for the collective mind, represents the cosmic imagination - the birthing place of the ideas behind the multifarous forms of creation that unfold to become explicate in the material world. It is also the eternal source from which human imagination draws its inspiration.

The influence of Jupiter, the previous ruler of the twelfth,[1] can also be felt here, bringing in qualities from the Sagittarius archetype to merge with the Pisces energy. Accordingly the twelfth house is known as the house of monasteries and hermitages - places under the auspices of the church where, freed from worldly responsibilities, we can devote ourself to spirituality.

But monasteries are also places where personal sacrifices are made, and sacrifice and surrender are the subject matter of Neptune and the Pisces archetype. Hence also the correlation between the twelfth house and prisons and hospitals, where we have no choice but to suffer restraint, and bow to the will of others. Surrender is also required when we are old and decrepit. On entering a care home,

---

1 Before Neptune was discovered in 1846, Jupiter was seen as the ruler of the Pisces archetype.

for example, we give up the control over our life and enter a set-up where we must to a large extent surrender our personal will. The twelfth house, of course, corresponds in the human life cycle to the final stage of senility and death.

The Three Heavenly Messengers

As our mental and physical powers dwindle in our dotage, life becomes narrower in scope. And, whether or not we are old when we enter the twelfth house with a Saturn transit, we could be weakened in some way and our scope could be narrowed by circumstances. For example, we could suffer a form of physical or mental disablement, or, feeling overpowered by adverse circumstances, we could simply shut down. Then we enter a limbo state in which the normal everyday routines that we rely on to give our life structure, fall apart, and we feel helpless to prevent this happening.

Attempting to resist this downturn is like King Canute trying to stop the tide from coming in. Resistance of any kind will only exacerbate the situation, and lead to more suffering. But, as Job of Old Testament fame discovered, patience is all. And at times when calamities strike and miseries reign down, the normal pain of living can reach a pitch of intensity at which it becomes the threshhold for spiritual breakthrough.

Buddha spoke of the 'three heavenly messengers' - referring to old age, disease and death, and in the twelfth house one or more of these characters can cross our path. Encounters with the heavenly messengers, however, should be welcomed as they transform us through provoking crises of meaning. In making us confront those uncomfortable truths about human life we prefer not to see, they cause us to ask some ultimate questions. And if, when we meet the messengers, we happen to be old and approaching the end of our days, they bring the glad tidings that heaven is drawing near.

All in all, how we react to our drowning in the twelfth house depends on whether or not we have successfully completed our labours in the previous houses. If we have faced our challenges and learned our lessons, our labours will have prepared us for this our final labour through raising our consciousness, and relocating us from our seat in the ego to our home at the centre of our being.

Balancing the Karmic Books

The law of karma is respected in the East as the basic moral law of a just universe. It ordains that all our deeds are weighed in the balance and, whether they occurred in this life or in past lives, wrong actions must be paid for. Christians call wrongdoing sin, and those who are on a secular path and have moral principles agree with them that the consequence of wrong doing is suffering in some form.

According to Eastern philosophy, if we are the victim of cruel treatment by others, this indicates that we ourself have been cruel in a like way in the past, because the law of karma decrees that we suffer a pain similar to that which we inflicted on others.

Only when the roles have been exchanged, and we have become victim instead of perpetrator, are we able to fully understand the harm we have done. So it seems suffering is needed in order to learn, and pain is a necessary precondition for the growth of consciousness. During the long process of suffering the consequences of our wrong doing, that can extend over many lives, our hearts are softened and we become compassionate. Thus the evolving universe is continuously being refined to a higher level of beauty, justice and coherence.

Knowing about the law of karma can be a help if we have Saturn in our twelfth house - either lifelong in our birthchart or for two and half years in transit. Then, if we are feeling like one of life's victims, we can find comfort in the thought that we are paying our karmic debts once and for all. But, if we are unaware of the law of karma, our fate may well appear to us as undeserved, and then we could magnify our suffering by becoming angry and railing against it.

Although we may have forgotten our past unjust actions, the universe never forgets. According to ancient wisdom, records not only of our deeds but also of our dreams, thoughts and imaginings are kept in the Akashic records that are held in the memory field of our planet. Now, in the twelfth house, our past returns to haunt us because, at this last stage on our journey round the wheel of life, we must finish our unfinished business, and let the past go through having a closure with it.

The twelfth is also known as the house of self-undoing because, on a deeper level, all our suffering is self-inflicted. If we do wrong, somewhere inside we are going to feel guilty, even if we are in denial. Thus we go on carrying repressed guilt feelings for lives on end. It is in order to shed this burden by balancing the books that we create suffering for ourself, albeit unconsciously. So someone who thinks he is a sinner will punish himself by inviting tribulation into his life.

The insight that on a deeper level we have chosen our suffering can change our attitude towards it, and bring a spiritual breakthrough. When we start taking responsibility for what happens to us in life, we leave the victim role behind. And, instead of continuing to nurse our grievances and play the martyr, we are ready to accept and forgive.

Like Blotting Paper

If we have the sun in the twelfth house in our birth chart, we will have many qualities in common with a Pisces. Jupiter will give us a happy-go-lucky approach to living, which can slip into a kind of carelessness when we couldn't care less. We will be attracted to boundless open spaces and, with our 'don't fence me in' attitude, must feel free in relationships to go as well as to come.

Neptune our ruler gives us heightened intuition and sensitivity, deepening our experience of the inner life, so we come to understand more about the human soul. These qualities can make us into good therapists or counsellors, as we look as deeply into others as we look into ourself. But there is a downside, as we can be hyper-sensitive and as porous as blotting paper. Then we indiscriminately absorb all the spilt ink around us, and become over-saturated.

Our porousness means we can take in from our environment emotions that are heavy and destabilising, which cause dark moods in us and volatile feeling states - unless, that is, we have learned the art of emotional detachment in the previous water houses. Another lesson we have hopefully learned is how to protect our space, because it will be hard to learn this in the twelfth house, where our perception of boundaries is so weak that we feel we have lost our contours, and are uncertain where we end and other people begin.

Opening up to the subtle energies within us and without us enriches our life experience, but it can also confuse and overwhelm us. If we appear to others as absent and lost in a world of our own, it may be because we are preoccupied with absorbing all the vibrations and resonances buzzing through the room. When we are in company, we can soon reach a point where we become stressed and over-stimulated. Then we must disappear and be alone to recuperate.

Like a fish leaving the choppy surface water and swimming down to the dark, silent depths, we can also escape by disappearing inside. Then we are absent to others though physically present. Our attention has turned away from the outer world to focus on our inner life, which we will usually find more fascinating. This is not always escapism as we need to plumb the depths to find solutions. Thus, when we have problems with another, our way is to withdraw rather than to discuss, as we need to be alone to listen to the answers that come from levels deeper than the mind.

The doorway to the collective unconscious is always a little ajar in the twelfth house, allowing the flow of transpersonal images and ideas to encroach on our mind. When we are meditating, we often notice negative emotions and painful images passing through that seem to have nothing to do with our personal story. So we should not necessarily own every image that comes into our head, especially those that are unsettling and make us anxious, as they may belong to the collective rather than to ourself.

Some twelfth-house people, however, intentionally plunge into the sea of the collective unconscious by taking mind-altering drugs. Their trips may excite and enthrall them, and give them extreme and bizarre inner experience, but they may over-estimate their capacity to process and integrate all they experience, and so become mentally unbalanced.

Recognising Which Way is Up

Contrary to expectations, a twelfth-house sun does not always preclude worldly success. For example, it appears a good placement for successful politicians, as proved by Margaret Thatcher, Helmut Kohl, George Bush and Tony Blair, who all have the sun in the twelfth. An explanation could be that as planets in the twelfth house are invisible, having the sun there allows them to keep their real selves and authentic attitudes out of sight. Twelfth-house people also have a chameleon-like quality and acting skills. So, perhaps these prime ministers and president manipulated their way into their positions of power by using their Neptunian subtlety to feel the pulse of the electorate, and to appear to the public in the most welcome guise.

A twelfth-house sun can also bring success to artists, actors, composers or people in advertising because it gives them the ability to instinctively fall in tune with current taste and values. And poets, painters and musicians with their sun here rise to fame through drawing inspiration from the archetypal level of the collective unconscious, and are thus able to produce work that touches the public deeply.

But there is a price to pay. A twelfth-house sun makes us vulnerable to collective feeling. Then our hearts will bleed with the victims of the human tragedies reported on the news, and we may find violent films or tear-jerkers too upsetting to watch. We could also be haunted by images of warfare or natural disasters in remote parts of the world, and suffer from recurring nightmares and irrational fears.

Doctors will then prescribe us drugs for what they see as physical disorders, and some twelfth-house people develop life-long addictions to their medication. Others dull their senses with alcohol or recreational drugs. Then, instead of going into therapy to sort themselves out, or finding a spiritual path to give them comfort and a purpose, they self-destruct.

The alcoholic or drug addict gets caught in a vicious circle as the more he drinks or drugs himself the more his inner life oppresses him. Then he needs to drink even more or take larger doses of his drug to blot it out and reach a state of oblivion. Instead of an evolutionary path, these people have chosen a path of spiritual devolution leading deeper and deeper into unconsciousness. And some will need to fall right to the bottom of the pile and become human derilicts before they can recognise which way is up.

Hidden Enemies

Saturn arriving in transit in the twelfth appears like a zen master with a zen stick. If we are being dreamy or feckless, up in the clouds or away with the fairies, he will give us a hit on the head that shocks us awake. Then, as the hidden enemies that are traditionally assigned to the twelfth emerge from their hiding places, he has his ways of forcing us to confront them. These enemies can manifest as people or outer circumstances that cripple us, or take the form of our own inner self-destructive urges.

When we are faced with overwhelming odds, the twelfth-house way is not to fight but to give up. However this kind of giving up is not surrender in a spiritual sense because it is not total. Instead it takes the form of passive resistance. Then, instead of being relaxed and accepting of our situation, we are tense with suppressed anger as we see ourself as a victim. Anger denied an outlet saps our life force, making us even more passive. So, feeling tired all the time, we become increasingly inert.

One method Saturn uses to shake us out of this condition is to conjure up a physical or mental health crisis. For example, our depression becomes so severe that we are unable to go to work, and have to accept that we are ill. We seek medical help, and our condition is diagnosed and we are prescribed cognitive therapy, which succeeds in making us aware of the psychological problems our depression was masking.

Another hidden enemy in the twelfth is the self-sabotaging urge that leads us to indiscriminately absorb everything that comes our way whether healthy or unhealthy. We become like dustbins into which people throw their garbage. Then Saturn is likely to throw something so unpleasant our way, that we wake up to what we are doing to ourself. We may recognise that we have a pattern of being attracted to people who are bad for us, and break off our relationships with them. The more we take responsibility for the way we allow others to treat us, the more we show we value ourself. And finally we come to value ourself too highly to allow others to abuse us.

Saturn in the twelfth can also indicate that we are on a mission that involves self-sacrifice. In this case we may voluntarily brave all kinds of hell on earth to serve our cause. Not only Christianity but other world religions too advocate self-sacrifice in the service of mankind as a spiritual path. A natal Saturn in the twelfth can point to past lives in which we adhered to religions that taught self-abnegation. Therefore it is possibly the case that, before this life began, we made a vow to dedicate it to selfless service.

Our strong empathy for the sufferings of the sick and starving populations of the world may motivate us to travel to a third world country to do charity work. Here we experience Neptune's boundlessness in the form of the bottomless pit of human suffering. The more starving children we feed, the more hungry mouths appear, and we feel our impotence in the face of the magnitude of these people's problems. This experience could throw us into a metaphysical crisis in which another powerful hidden enemy could emerge - the monster despair.

Or we come to trust that in a greater framework of meaning suffering on this scale also has a purpose, as the universe is intelligent, conscious and benign. We do our bit, though it seems to be merely a drop in the ocean, and then surrender and let be.

The Raindrop Returns to the Ocean

In this final house on the wheel of life, our path leads into aloneness. This will not necessarily be our choice but circumstances will throw us back on ourself. Try as we may, we cannot avoid confronting our fear of loneliness. However when we experience loneliness in its depths, we discover that we have been hoodwinked by yet another self-limiting belief.

Aloneness is not loneliness when there is no longing for the other. Then it is a positive rather than a negative state. It is generous as it gives us space at last to explore our inner world. Aloneness is also a temple made for practising meditation, which is to fulfil the highest potential of the twelfth house.

Through meditating we learn to centre ourself in the core of our being. There we tap into a source of Herculean strength. It will equip us to take on all kinds of inner monsters - the formidable two-headed dog we must slay before rounding up our cattle, and Geryon, the terrible three-bodied monster, who we defeat with the arrow of our unflinching purpose. Geryon represents our deepest and strongest fear. But, once he is slain, we can start our ascent into the Alps, driving our cattle before us. They represent the unconscious and wandering parts of our mind, and we will need the strong hand of an alert consciousness to keep them from straggling and falling into an abyss. Thus, we cross the Alps, representing life's hardships and austerities, to arrive home with them in triumph.

Hercules paid his karma by surrendering to King Eurystheus, and agreeing to perform the labours he demanded. Like Hercules we must follow life wherever it leads in the twelfth house, as life is not going to follow us. If we have other ideas or we are resistive, suffering and limitation will be our lot. Our labour is therefore to surrender to the will of the whole. But this requires a trust that we only find when the monsters of our fears and negative beliefs have been overcome. Then we will see the love and compassion that was always in our heart, but which our fears had overshadowed, reflected in a loving and caring universe.

The raindrop returning to the ocean is a Buddhist image for enlightenment. As it melts into the waves it surrenders its separateness. However, instead of making us poorer, this loss makes us richer, because it is through losing its self that the raindrop gains the whole ocean.

Appendix I

The aim of this section of the book is to help the reader distinguish the archetypes as they appear in the wheel of the houses. I list the main qualities in a table, and then give key-words for the circumstances and personality qualities that the archetype is likely to call forth. There is a field of potential meaning around each archetype that is likely to manifest, in this case, in the respective house. But it may not. We have a choice in the way the archetypes express in our life, as we are participators in the creative unfolding of the universe.

The First House Archetype

Sign	Aries
Planet	Mars
Element	fire
Humour	hot and dry
House Type	angular
Mode	cardinal
Colour	bright red
Labour	Taming the Wild Mares of Diomedes

Traditional subject matter: the self, vitality, physical appearance, outlook on life

Modern themes: fresh start, drive, impetus to action, severance, identity, conflict, persona

First-house weaknesses: destructive anger, wilful, impatient, self-serving, inconsiderate, rash, aggressive, violent

First-house strengths: great energy, assertiveness, resilience, pioneering, forceful, bold, decisive, innocence, authentic

The Second House Archetype

Sign	Taurus
Planet	Venus
Element	earth
Humour	cold and dry
House type	succedent
Mode	fixed
Colour	leaf green and pink
Labour	Capturing the Cretan Bull

Traditional subject matter: Body, money, movable possessions, resources, expenditure, creature comforts

Modern themes: mother earth, the provider, material resources, body-image, sustenance, material security, territory, values

Second-house weaknesses: greedy, possessive, stubborn, complacent, lazy, self-indulgent, covetous, hoarding

Second-house strengths: ability to ground, sustain and provide, practicality, pragmatism, beauty, sensuality, love, peace

The Third House Archetype

Sign	Gemini
Planet	Mercury
Element	air
Humour	Hot and moist
House type	cadent
Mode	mutable
Colour	yellow
Labour	Gathering the Golden Apples of the Hesperides

Traditional subject matter: communication, siblings, neighbours, neighbourhood, schools, retail trade, short journeys, news

Modern themes: duality, intellect, ideas, media, local contacts, perception, education, dexterity

Third-house weaknesses: flippant, superficial, a mine of useless information, a chatterbox, fickle, inconsistent, restless

Third-house strengths: logical, lucid, articulate, curious, witty, knowledgeable, versatile, flexible, quick-witted, amusing

The Fourth House Archetype

Sign	Cancer
Planet	Moon
Element	water
Humour	cold and moist
House type	angular
Mode	cardinal
Colour	silver
Labour	Capturing the Golden-Antlered Doe

Traditional subject matter: parents, ancestors, landed property, beginning and end of life, boats, the sea, retirement

Modern Themes: past, origins, home, psychological inheritance, childhood, mother (or father), mother-child pattern, private life, nurturing, personal unconscious, emotions, personal psyche

Fourth-house weaknesses: clinging, dependent, moody, over-sensitive, needy, self-pitying,

Fourth-house strengths: motherly, nurturing, caring, home-maker, tender, protective, sympathetic, intuitive, empathetic

The Fifth House Archetype

Sign	Sun
Planet	Leo
Element	fire
Humour	hot and dry
Mode	fixed
House type	succedent
Colour	gold
Labour	Slaying the Nemean Lion

Traditional subject matter: children, sports, recreation, love affairs, pleasures, accomplishments, speculation

Modern themes: the hero, procreation, creative self-expression, raising children, self-confidence, self-mastery, power

Fifth-house weaknesses: conceited, arrogant, dominating, vain, autocratic, overbearing, flamboyant, supercilious

Fifth-house strengths: creative, charistmatic, life-affirmative, loyal, masterful, strong, noble, generous, big-hearted

The Sixth House Archetype

Sign	Virgo
Planet	Mercury
Element	earth
Humour	cold and dry
Mode	mutable
House type	cadent
Colour	dark green
Labour	Seizing Hippolyte's Girdle

Traditional subject matter: health, daily chores, servants and employees, co-workers, work place, household pets

Modern themes: service, daily routine, adjustment, purity, perfection, healing, practical skills

Sixth-house weaknesses: over-critical, narrowly rational, fastidious, sceptical, worrying, control-freak

Sixth-house strengths: clean and neat, modest, efficient, methodical, meticulous, helpful, practical, orderly

The Seventh House Archetype

Sign	Libra
Planet	Venus
Element	air
Humour	hot and moist
Mode	cardinal
House type	angular
Colour	sky blue
Labour	Capturing the Erymanthian Boar

Traditional subject matter: marriage, partnerships (domestic, legal and commercial), the lower courts, contracts, open adversaries

Modern themes: One-to-one relationships, our opposite number, the type we find attractive, our relationship pattern, justice

Seventh-house weaknesses: prevaricating, giving double messages, indecisive, ingratiating, two-faced, over conciliatory

Seventh-house strengths: creating beauty and harmony, cultured, caring and supportive of partners, cooperative, fair, socially aware, diplomatic, accommodating, peace-loving

The Eighth House Archetype

Sign	Scorpio
Planet	Pluto (Mars)
Element	water
Humour	cold and wet
Mode	fixed
House type	succedent
Colour	dark red
Labour	Destroying the Hydra of Lerna

Traditional subject matter: Death, inheritance, taxes, other people's money and values, wills

Modern themes: debts, mortgages, sex, degeneration, repressed feelings, therapy, parapsychology

Eighth-house weaknesses: secretive, scheming, unscrupulous, obsessive, jealous, grudging, vindictive, revengeful

Eighth-house strengths: passionate, brave, loyal, totally involved, compassionate, high ideals, determined, committed

The Ninth House Archetype

Sign	Sagittarius
Planet	Jupiter
Element	fire
Humour	hot and dry
Mode	mutable
House type	cadent
Colour	purple
Labour	Overcoming the Stymphalian birds

Traditional subject matter: The church, priests, universities, higher courts, long-distance travel, in-laws

Modern themes: foreign countries and cultures, higher education, ethics, belief systems

Ninth-house weaknesses: boisterous, impatient, excessive, extravagant, slapdash, over-the-top, judgemental, unreliable, proselytising

Ninth-house strengths: adventurous, inspiring, benevolent, liberal, tolerant, jovial, enthusiastic, lucky, frank, freedom-loving, optimistic, high-minded

The Tenth House Archetype

Sign	Capricorn
Planet	Saturn
Element	earth
Humour	cold and dry
Mode	cardinal
House type	angular
Colour	brown
Labour	Overcoming Cerberus and freeing Prometheus

Traditional subject matter: career, the public arena, reputation, status, public position, mother or father, government, institutions

Modern themes: authority figures, limits, structure, supports, law and order, responsibility, achievements, worldly ambition

Tenth-house weaknesses: proud, severe, austere, heavy-handed, hard, autocratic, rigid, disciplinarian, wet blanket, conservative

Tenth-house strengths: self-reliant, upright, steadfast, disciplined, responsible, patient, stoical, efficient, productive

The Eleventh House Archetype

Sign	Aquarius
Planet	Uranus (Saturn)
Element	air
Humour	hot and moist
Mode	fixed
House type	succedent
Colour	indigo
Labour	Cleansing the Augean Stables

Traditional subject matter: friends and acquaintances, societies, groups, political parties, associations, clubs, future visions

Modern themes: social goals and objectives, causes, radical ideas, revolution, group ideals, alternative and progressive movements

Eleventh-house weaknesses: eccentric, unpredictable, defiant, reckless, rebellious, fanatical, disruptive, overwrought

Eleventh-house strengths: original, idealistic, unconventional, innovative, humanitarian, high-minded, dispassionate, committed

The Twelfth House Archetype

Sign	Pisces
Planet	Neptune (Jupiter)
Element	water
Humour	cold and moist
Mode	mutable
House type	cadent
Colour	aquamarine
Labour	Capturing the Cattle of Geryon

Traditional subject matter: hospitals, prisons, monasteries, hermitages, charity, secret enemies, self-undoing, seclusion

Modern themes: the collective unconscious, karma, guilt, suffering, sacrifice and service, mystical visions, spiritual awakening

Twelfth-house weaknesses: martyr, dreamer, drifter, compulsive helper, escapist, self-destructive, dissipated, addiction prone, evasive

Twelfth-house strengths: empathy, compassion, gentleness, trust sensitivity, psychic skills, selfless service, spirituality

Appendix II

Signs	Houses	Ruling Planets
Aries	1	Mars
Taurus	2	Venus
Gemini	3	Mercury
Cancer	4	Moon
Leo	5	Sun
Virgo	6	Mercury
Libra	7	Libra
Scorpio	8	Pluto (Mars)
Sagittarius	9	Jupiter
Capricorn	10	Saturn
Aquarius	11	Uranus (Saturn)
Pisces	12	Neptune (Jupiter)

LEBENSRAD – WHEEL OF LIFE

An Astrology Board Game by Phoebe Wyss

Follow in the footsteps of Hercules and perform your twelve labours as you move round horoscope through the houses, each of which stands for an archetypal field of experience. The synchronicities are striking when you play this oracle game. The planets you take with closed eyes, and the sentences on the task-cards the dice leads you to, are likely to be very relevant to your life, and may bring new insights. When the game is played with friends and family, conversations arise about things that really matter. Thus, through playing Lebensrad, you learn more about astrology, more about yourself and more about others.

For more information and to order see
www.astrophoebe.com

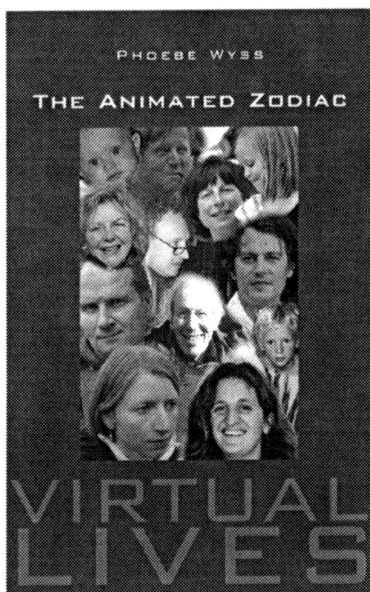

PHOEBE WYSS

THE ANIMATED ZODIAC

VIRTUAL
LIVES

Virtual Lives: The Animated Zodiac by Phoebe Wyss

This entertaining and informative book about the human condition brings the twelve archetypes to life in fictional form. Twelve souls meet with their life-coach in the inter-life to prepare for incarnation. They are allocated different zodiac signs, giving them different personalities and different challenges to face. The reader, who accompanies them from cradle to grave, is given a direct experience of what it is like to be in the skin of other people. The stories in this original self-help book do more than describe twelve different life paths and personality profiles. They suggest answers to some ultimate questions.

To be published Autumn 2007
by Tree Tongue Publishing. Order your copy now from
www.astrophoebe.com